Mrs Cromwell's C

THE
COURT & KITCHEN
OF
ELIZABETH,

Commonly called

Joan Cromwell,

THE
Wife of the Late Usurper

Originally printed by Thomas Milbourn
for Randal Taylor in St Martin-le-Grand, London, 1664

Recipes from the wife of Oliver Cromwell

Introduction by Stuart Orme

From feigned glory & Usurped Throne
And all the Greatnesse to me falsly shown
And from the Arts of Government set free
See how Protectresse & a Drudge agree

THE COURT & KITCHIN OF ELIZABETH,

Commonly called
Joan Cromwel,
THE
Wife of the late Usurper;

Truly
Described and Represented,

And now
Made Publick for general
Satisfaction.

London, Printed by *Tho. Milbourn,* for *Randal Taylor* in
St. *Martins Le Grand,* 1664.

THE
Cromwell
MUSEUM

ISBN 978-1-913663-79-7

Printed in Great Britain by
Biddles Books Limited, King's Lynn, Norfolk

Introduction

On display in the Cromwell Museum in Huntingdon is a small, unassuming looking volume; a leather bound book with aged printed pages, the title of which proclaims it to be *"The Court and Kitchen of Elizabeth, Commonly Called Joan Cromwell, the Wife of the Late Usurper."* The appearance of the book belies its significance as one of the strangest cookery books ever published; it claims to contain the personal recipes collected by Oliver Cromwell's wife Elizabeth. These are bound in a volume together with an extended introduction composed of essays condemning the Cromwellian regime in general, the evils of its court and targeting Elizabeth in particular.

Copy of the cookery book displayed in the Cromwell Museum

The volume has 102 recipes which might have been common in the mid-1600s and is a fascinating window into the food and dining of the period as well as being relevant to several different areas of study.

Royalist Propaganda?

Published in 1664 under the restored Charles II, on first sight the book seems to be a piece of Royalist propaganda. The title applied the name 'Joan' to Elizabeth Cromwell not as she was known by this, but to be demeaning as it was a name often associated with common prostitutes. Implications of sexual impropriety were often used in 17th century pamphlets to condemn notable women.

Another line of attack in the book was to portray Elizabeth as a parsimonious housekeeper *"a hundred times fitter for a barn than a palace"*. There as a deeper meaning to this, by saying that she was not able to run an efficient large household, so it implied that her husband would be unable to run the country. As elsewhere in history, the running of a prudent household was often equated with the efficient government of the nation. The recipes included Fenland ingredients like eels, thus adding to the rather snobbish implication that the Cromwells were far too ordinary and therefore unsuited to rule.

A number of accusations are made in the initial essays about the way that Elizabeth and her husband ran their court; many of these can be disproven thanks to the exhaustive work conducted by the historian Roy Sherwood in his volumes *'The Court of Oliver Cromwell'* and *'Oliver Cromwell: King in All But Name'*. Whilst accusations of thriftiness can be borne out those relating to the widespread dismissal of staff, most particularly the cook Philip Stafford, can be shown to have been the invention of the introduction's writer.

The volume can be seen as part of the proliferation of printed propaganda materials that had developed during and after the Civil War. Before then there had been strict government regulation and censorship of any printed materials, but once war broke out this control disappeared, and huge quantities of print were produced. In 1642 more printed material was published than had been in the preceding 165 years since the printing press arrived in England. Both sides used printing as a means of spreading propaganda with no form of control, which was increasingly effective at a time when perhaps a third of the population was literate.

Printed newsbooks reported the news as it came in, so were not printed regularly like modern newspapers. However, they were often lurid, politically biased and reported rumour as fact (claiming defeats as victories for example) to get their message across and to sell as many copies as possible. Although censorship had been reintroduced under the Commonwealth, the genie was out of the bottle, and the state continued to use similar methods too. After the Restoration in 1660 printed materials proliferated to denigrate the Cromwellian regime and promote the restored monarchy's legitimacy, of which this book is a clear example.

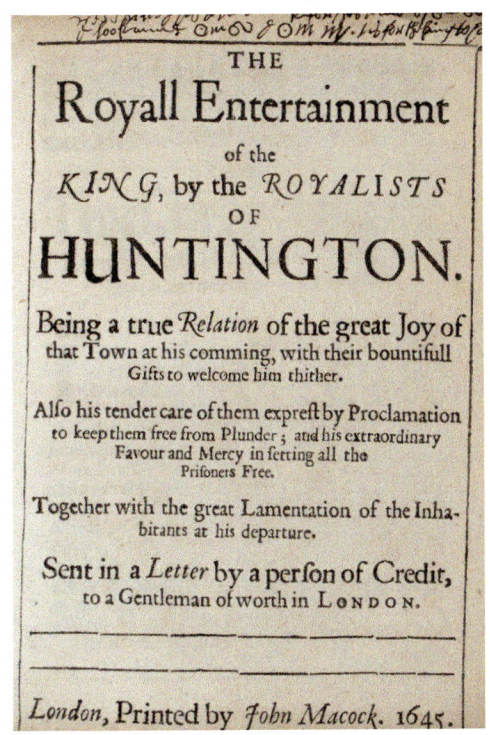

Parliamentarian newsbook alleging Royalist war crimes committed during their occupation of Huntingdon in 1645.

What does it tell us about Elizabeth Cromwell?

Despite her importance in Cromwell's story, there are large gaps in what we know about his wife Elizabeth. We know that she was born as Elizabeth Bourchier in 1598, the eldest of twelve children (nine sons and three daughters) of Sir James Bourchier and his wife Frances. Sir James had inherited land and property from his father before becoming a successful businessman in his own right in the London fur and leather trades. He owned property in the City of London around Tower Hill, and in Essex including Little Stambridge Hall and was knighted by James I at his coronation in July 1603. We know nothing about Elizabeth's childhood, though she must have received some sort of education as we know from her surviving correspondence that she was literate.

Elizabeth's life is something of a mystery until her marriage to Oliver Cromwell in 1620. How the couple met is unknown, although there are several possibilities. Sir James Bourchier was knighted at the same time as Sir Oliver Cromwell, Oliver's uncle and godfather, at King James I's coronation. It may have been through another family link, as Elizabeth's aunt was married to another of Oliver's uncles. It has been suggested that Cromwell moved in Essex society and may have met the Bourchiers through this, or that he spent some time in London after the death of his father in 1617 and met them then.

By whatever means Oliver Cromwell and Elizabeth Bourchier met, and whether it was love or arranged match, they were married at St Giles Church, Cripplegate on 20 August 1620. The Cromwells seem to have been a devoted family, despite the ups and downs of their fortunes; from a comfortable existence in Huntingdon to living in reduced circumstances in St Ives. Oliver Cromwell was plunged into a period of 'melancholia', widely interpreted as depression during this period, before developing a deep faith within the 'Godly' movement known to us popularly as Puritans. From the references in her surviving letter Elizabeth seems to have become similarly devout.

An inheritance in 1636, including a substantial house in Ely, provided for them comfortably. That house survives and is open to the public as Oliver Cromwell's House, including a lovely kitchen which has barely changed from that time. It is interesting to speculate whether any of the recipes within the *'Court and Kitchen'* were prepared in that space.

The couple had 9 children; one, James, died in infancy, whilst their two oldest sons Robert and Oliver both died after barely reaching manhood. Whilst these changes and losses must have put a strain on their relationship, there is no serious suggestion that either of the Cromwells strayed from the marriage bed, and judging by their few surviving letters to each other they had obviously developed a deep affection. Cromwell wrote to Elizabeth from on campaign in Scotland in 1650, telling her:

> *"Thou art dearer to me than any creature; let that suffice... My Dearest, I could not satisfy myself to omit this post, although I have not much to write; yet indeed I love to write to my dear, who is very much in my heart. It joys me to hear thy soul prospereth; the Lord increase His favours to thee more and more...The Lord bless all thy good counsel and example to all those about thee, and hear all thy prayers, and accept thee always".*

Elizabeth responded:

> *"Truly my life is but half a life in your absence, did not the Lord make it up in himself, which I must acknowledge to the praise of his grace".*

18th century portrait of Oliver Cromwell, one of a pair

Mrs Cromwell's Cookbook

18th century portrait of Elizabeth Cromwell, one of a pair

During the Civil War, and Cromwell's resulting rise to prominence from relative obscurity as a minor MP to a senior officer and key figure in Parliament, the family seem to have spent an increasing time in London. The introduction to the *'Court and Kitchen'* suggests that their residence became a hotbed of political activity, that:

> "...*her House was in this respect a political or State Exchange by which the Affairs of the Kingdom were governed, and the prizes of all things set, whether Offices, preferments, Indemnity; as all other manner of Collusion and Deceits were practised, and money stirring nowhere else...*"

The insinuation that there was corruption involved is unsubstantiated, but Elizabeth was accused of intrigue in some contemporary pamphlets. Nineteenth Century historians disagreed on the issue of how much influence she had on her husband, some suggesting that she was a spur to his ambitions, others that she limited herself to domestic matters. Certainly in her one surviving letter she reminded Cromwell that he needed to keep certain political allies informed as to his activities, but as the evidence is so limited we cannot really say for certain how much Elizabeth was involved in such matters.

By the 1650s Elizabeth and her family were living in lodgings adjoining Whitehall Palace, in a wing known as the Cock Pit. In the Spring of 1654, after her husband became Lord Protector, they moved into newly redecorated apartments in Whitehall Palace and at Hampton Court. She was now the wife of the head of state, accorded the title 'Her Highness the Lady Protectress'. Elizabeth played a minor and supporting role in some public occasions, especially entertaining the wives and daughters of ambassadors and other dignitaries, but otherwise seems to have stayed in the background, and she was neither assigned nor seems to have sought real power or a political role.

Portrait of Elizabeth Cromwell as Lady Protectoress by Robert Walker, c.1655

At Cromwell's death in 1658 Elizabeth was well provided for, with an annuity and lodgings in St James'. The Restoration in 1660 left her position more uncertain and she left London. Newsbooks accused of her of trying to remove royal property *Information being given that there were several of his Majesty's goods at a fruiterer's warehouse near the Three Cranes... which were there kept as the goods of Mrs. Eliz. Cromwell, wife to Oliver Cromwell, deceased... it being not very improbable that the said Mrs. Cromwell might convey away some such goods..."*

Elizabeth strenuously denied these accusations, and petitioned Charles II, stressing that she had played no role in the public affairs of the previous years, professing obedience to the new regime and requesting that: *"after the many sorrows wherewith it hath pleased the all wise God to exercise'* her, she might be allowed *'a safe retirement... now in her old age".*

Despite her concerns, Elizabeth was able to retire quietly to lodge with her widowed son-in-law John Claypole at Northborough Manor, just on the north side of Peterborough. She was visited by her children on occasion, who expressed concern at her increasing ill-health, until she died in November 1665, and was buried in the local church.

17th Century Cookery Books

Despite its status as a propaganda tool, the *'Court and Kitchen'* was far from unique in being a cookery book published in the 1600s. Indeed, it can be contrasted with a very similar volume published in 1655 *'The Queen's Closet Opened'* which allegedly took recipes and remedies from the exiled Queen Mother, Henrietta Maria. She had been unpopular in England before the Civil Wars for being both French and Roman Catholic. The volume, almost certainly written by her private secretary Walter Montagu, was a means of reinventing the Queen's image as the 'mother of the nation' by showing her domestic competence, thus making her more relatable. It directly contrasts with the *'Court and Kitchen'* in many respects, idealising the Queen as a wife and mother and therefore reinforcing the Stuart's dynasty's fitness to rule as opposed to the upstart Cromwells.

Frontispiece of 'The Queen's Closet Opened', 1668 edition

These books were part of a growing trend for domestic manuals and cookery books, fuelled by increased literacy, more cost-effective printing, and an expanding affluent middle class hungry for such volumes. In 1615 Gervase Markham had published *'The English Housewife'*, a compendium of household advice and the Mrs Beeton of its day. The other oft-quoted cookery book from this period was the *'Closet Opened'* of Sir Kenelm Digby, published in 1669, a collection of recipes which is arguably the first 'foodie's cookbook'. Robert May, the mid-17th century equivalent of a celebrity chef, published what is arguably the first 'modern' cookery book in 1660, *'The Accomplish't Cook'*, which is organised into specific and logical sections as opposed to be being a collection of recipes in no particular order. Critics have often decried the *'Court and Kitchen'* for having no logical order to it, but this was the norm for this period.

Like most other cookbooks of the period, the recipes in the *'Court and Kitchen'* only contain the 'method' (in modern terms) part of the recipe; no ingredients list or cooking time is included. This was because ingredients would need to be more flexible depending what was available regionally or seasonally and given the limitations of food preservation at the time. Cooking times would also vary, not least depending on the facilities available in each household, generally using an open fire to cook or roast over.

Food and Dining in the 1600s

To get a better understanding of the recipes contained with the *'Court and Kitchen'*, it is worth saying a little about the nature of food and dining in this period. Generally, most people would consume three meals per day, if they could afford it: Breakfast, Dinner and Supper. Of these breakfast and supper would usually be light meals of a single course at each end of the day, whilst the main meal would be consumed around 12noon – 2pm, depending on the season. This might consist of two or more courses, each of which would contain several dishes. There was not the distinction at this time of sweet and savoury tastes, and these might be mixed in courses or even dishes to suit the Early Modern palate. Cutlery was becoming recognisable to that used today; by the 1600s the fork was now being widely used by the English for the first time, having resisted its use for centuries as it was widely believed to be a French invention. The quality and materials used in dining-ware reflected one's status in society, with those aspiring to gentility eating off pewter and drinking from glassware; the poorest eating from wooden plates and drinking from horn cups.

Ingredients varied regionally (such as the Fenland Eels in the *'Court and Kitchen'*) and seasonally, although certain items could be dried, salted, or pickled to aid preservation. Certain ingredients that we might think of as being expensive today were regarded as commonplace, even peasant food at the time, such as salmon and

Engraving of a busy 17th century kitchen

oysters. Although potatoes were now known in England they were not widely eaten; bread was still regarded as the staple part of the diet. Spices were widely used in many recipes less, as the common misconception has it, to take away the taste of poorly preserved food, but to add different tastes to the food and as a symbol of status and conspicuous consumption with their expense. Cooking tended to be done by pot cooking over an open fire ('pottage'), roasting on a spit, or baking in a brick oven for pies, pastries, and bread. Whilst cooking at home was deemed to be the province of womenfolk, the housewife or female servants, professional cooks in great households or eating establishments tended to be exclusively men.

Dining out was common in this period, both as a social activity and to avoid the necessity of cooking at home. This could involve eating at inns and taverns, but also by buying pies or pastries amongst other things as a form of 'fast food'. One development of the Cromwellian period was the growth of Coffee Houses, the first of which in London was opened in 1652 by Pasqua Rosee.

Conclusions

A key question that most visitors to the Cromwell Museum who look at the book ask is 'did the Cromwell family really use these recipes'? It is impossible to know for sure, and many writers have dismissed the volume as being clearly designed as a piece of political propaganda, and that therefore the recipes could have come from anywhere. On the other hand, there are small personal details in the book which are consistent and credible with what we know about the Cromwell family, and the recipes fit with a family of their social background; the 'middling sort' recipes available in the mid-1600s.

The kitchen fireplace at Oliver Cromwell's House in Ely

Personally, I am inclined to think that at least some of these dishes were enjoyed by the Cromwell family themselves, although in one sense it does not matter whether they did or did not. This book is still a fascinating window into the culinary tastes, print culture and politics of one of the most tumultuous and fascinating periods in our history.

Stuart Orme
Curator, The Cromwell Museum

Mrs Cromwell's Cookbook

Note:

The text within this volume is from a new transcription undertaken by Cromwell Museum volunteer Joseph Chiswell in 2019, and we are very grateful for his time and effort in producing this.

It was transcribed from the original 1665 edition in the Cromwell Museum's collections.

Spelling and grammar have been retained as per the original edition.

THE COURT & KITCHIN OF *ELIZABETH*,

Commonly called

Joan Cromwel,

THE Wife of the Late Usurper,

Truly Described and Represented,

And now Made Publick for general Satisfaction.

London, Printed by *Tho. Milbourn*, for *Randal Taylor* in St. Martins Le Grand, 1664.

The Introductions

TO THE READER

THAT there may no prejudice lye against this Publication, as an insultory, unmanlike Invective and Triumph over the supposed miserable and forlorn estate of this Family, and this Person in particular; it will be requisite to obviate & prepare against the seeming humane (but indeed disloyal, or at least idle) sentiment and reverence to the frail and fluctuating condition of mankind, which as a general Argument is ready at hand to oppose the design of the ensuing Treatise.

    Not to refer the Reader to the practise of all Times, which have not failed to wreak the fury of the Pen upon Tyrants and Usurpers (if surviving to punishment, otherwise their Relations and Posterity) whole execrable Tragedies have wearied the World, and blunted the Instruments of death & slaughter: nor to instance the particular examples thereof, as sufficient Authority for this Imitation; the peculiar Justice due to the monstrous enormities and unparalle'ld insolence of these upstarts, (besides the disproportion and incompetence of any revenge to their provoking impudent personation of Princes) will interessedly vindicate and defend the Author from the breach of charity, much more from the rigid imputation and charge, as of a person devested and void of nature, compassion and civility.

    For while they yet wanton in the abundance of their spoyl & rapine, afflicted with nothing else but the torments of ambitious designs, taking this cloud upon them, but as an Eclipse of their former Greatness, and as but a Turn of sporting Fortune, whose wheel may with an imaginary volutation roll their pretty Highnesses upwards again; how can the desperate depressed estate of many thousand loyal Subjects , who are irrecoverably lost and past all means, but a miracle, to their just, or any competent Restitution, or to buoy up themselves or Families from vulgar or Phanatick contempt: How is it possible for them to comport with the Serenity (instead of disaster) of this Family, by whose single accursed plots and designs, all their present and many more grievous past miseries are derived upon them and their posterity.

And that this may not seem the froth and spleen of a Satyr, what meaneth that bleating in their present stately Mansions? The same ceremonious and respectful observances, as if they were still the *Hogen Mogens.*

None of the Family must presume to speak less than my Lord and my Lady, to the Squire *Henry* and his Spouse, and the same stile is used when ever any mention is made of them in the Household;

Portrait of Richard Cromwell by John Hayls, c. 1658

to which pin the neighbours and necessary Retainers addresses are tunably raised. What is this but to strengthen their weak, yet vain-glorious fancy, and to preserve some reliques of their former veneration, lest rude and inofficious time should plead a disuser in bar to their conceited (but airy) reversion? And no questionbut the old Gentlewoman, who took so much upon her, and was so well pleased with her last Grandeur, as displeased and afflicted with the fall of it, betwixt *Fleetwood*, *Richard* and *Desborough*, is also served in the same manner, and with the same Grandezza's, so that such is the inveterate itch and tetter of Honour in Her, that nothing but the lees of gall, and the most biting sharpest Ink will ere be able to cure or stop this *Protectorian Evil*.

And herein we do but retaliate (if they be not unworthy of such a term, as that any attribute of justice should be profaned by their demerit which exacts rather popular Fury) and repay them in some sort, those many Libels, blasphemous Pamphlets and Pasquils, broached and set on foot, chiefly by the late Usurper, against the blessed Memory and Honour of our two late sovereigns: more especially those vile and impious Pieces, called, *The Court and Character of King James*, and *The None Such Charles*, (a great number of which were brought up in the juncture of the late Restitution, (as particularly informed) which in the worst of times their bold and impudent falsehood made most abominable) were none of the least incentives to a work of this nature, in requital of that traiterous and most petulant Imposture.

Whereas the guilt of this *Grand-Dame* hath this sort of felicity, that it cannot be made worse or more odious by any additions of devised untruths; and he must be a very immodest and immoderate Fabulist that can represent Her to greater disadvantage in this way, then her Actions have infamed her to the World.

Her Highness must be pleased to dispense with this frank and libertine manner of treating Her, for 'tis all we are like to have for many millions; besides an old Saw or Proverb to the bargain,

— *Olim haec meminisse juvabit*; a little transitory mirth, for twenty years duration of sorrow; and if she thinks she comes not very well off so, she is unreasonable in her reduction and allowed Recess, (to be envied for its plenty and amplitude, far exceeding her former privacy, so that she is even yet a Darling of Fortuneo as in her usurped Estate and Greatness.

It is well for her, if his *Butchery* (then, which the Sun never saw a more flagitous execrable fact, and so comprehensive, that it reached *Caligulas* with) can be slighted into her cookery; and that there were no other *Monument* of it then in *Paste*,

— *Ut tantum schombros metuentia Crimina, vel Thus*: That the records of his Crimes were onely damn'd to an *Oven*. Little *satisfaction* serves the English Nation (the Relations of those loyal persons martyred by Him excepted) and She ought therefore to be highly thankful, that the *Scene* of his *Tyranny* was laid here, for had it light upon the *Southern parts* of the World, their *nimble* and *vindictive* rage, upon the *Turn*, would have *limb'd* and *minced* her Family to *Atomes*, and have been their own *Cooks* and *Carvers*.

Lambert Simnel very contentedly turned a broach in the Kings Kitchin, after the Gaudies of his Kingly Imposture, in the beginning of the reign of *Henry* the VII. and therefore for variety sake let this once mighty Lady, do *Drudgery* to the Publique.

Vale.

The Introduction.

Among al the monstrous Effects of *Cromwell's* Tyranny, and the fruition of his usurped Greatnesse; in the affluence of all imaginary delights to gratify his sense, and candy over the troubles of his mind (to the rendring them lesse severe and dulling their poignant acutenesse) it was by all men much wondred at, that he was so little guilty of any luxurious and Epicurean Excesses either in his meat or drink, except sometimes in his Cups, which he purposely and liberally took off to void the gravel in his Kidneys, with which he was continually molested, and for which, large draughts were his ordinary Cure.

In this He differed from the rest of his sanguinous Tribe and sort of men, who making use of humane blood for their drink, do saginate and fatten themselves with the superfluous variety of meats, to whose natural satisfaction such artificial devices are added (even retorturing the Creature) that the genunine Gusto is quite changed by this adulteration, and lost in the mixt multiplicity of other Relishes and palatable Ingredients. Herein like themselves, when not content with their natural private condition of life, and the pure results & simple innocent delights thereof, they do corrode their minds with the sharp sawces of Ambition, and so alter and invert their nature, that they degenerate to other things, and become such a *quel-que-chose* of villainy and debauchery, that we can hardly sever and distinguish a Crime which is intervitiated with many other. And what prodigious infamy upon this gulose ant and intemperate account, and by this very apt similitude doth this day stick upon many if not most of the *Roman* Emperors! as I could instance in *Tiberius, Caligula, Nero, Otho, Domitian, Commodus, Caracalla, Heliogabolus,* men not to be mentioned without horrour at their wickednesse; of such savage and feral manners, as if their food had been the flesh of *Panthers, Tygers* and *Bears,* and had assimilated its nutriment

Mrs Cromwell's Cookbook

Full length portrait of Oliver Cromwell by Robert Walker, c. 1649

in their Bestial qualities: but as was said before, *Cromwell* as in some other cases, was in this wholly discriminated from them.

Yet do I not think this abstemiousnesse and temperance was due only to his disposition either of body or mind, for his appetite in all other things was very irregular & inordinate, but either to the multitude of those *mordaces & edaces Curae*, biting and eating cares and ambitious thoughts; which made him either the Vulturs or *Tantalus* his Feast, and were his continual Surfets of an evil conscience;

Districtus Enfis cui super impia
Cervice pendet, non Siculae dapes
Dulcem elaborarint saporem
Horat, Od

though I may indulge his military labours and discipline, and Example that severer abstinence: or else which is principally intended here as the Subject matter of this discourse, it may be cheaplyer referred to the sordid frugality and thrifty baseness of his Wife, *Elizabeth Bowcher*, the daughter of Sir *James Bowcher*, commonly called Protectresse *Joan* and vulgarly known of later years by no other Christian name, even in the great Heighth of her Husbands power, and that chiefly out of Derision and contemptuous indignation, that such a person durst presume to take upon herself such a Soveraign Estate, when she was an hundred times fitter for a Barn than a Palace; so sporting, mocking Fate, to make good that of the Satyrist

Foelix à Tergo quem nulla Ciconia pinxit, followed her great luck with that Sarcastick and dicterious nickname, that she with her Copemate might perceive, their Fortune was not so entire and of so fair an aspect and firm Structure, but that the Flaws and Blemishes and Impotence thereof, were most obvious and ridiculous; their Fine

Feathers had Swans feet, and their beautiful Mermaid, the fiction of Dominion, had the ugly tail and fins of a Fish, the *Train* of her greatness and prosperity was the most vile and scornful reproaches. All this shall suffice to be spoken of her person by way of Preface, the next Elenchus or Discourse is of her Mesnagery Huswifery or House-keeping.

THE
Court *and* Kitchin
OF
Mrs. ELIZABETH
Alias
Joane Cromwell.

To Confine and limit this Treatise to its purpose and designment prefixed in the Title, we must (though with some petty injury to the Reader) pass over her Oeconomy at her private home, before *Olivers* bold atchievement of the Supreme power, (because part of it is already publique) when she had brought as (we say) a *Noble to Nine pence*, by her pious negligence and ill management of the Domestique Affairs, and was as giddy to see her bare Walls as *Oliver* was mad with *Enthusiasmes* and Devinations of Regal Furniture and all Princely pomp and greatness. Those Memorials may be reduced to this present use in this short Corollary.

That the former Extermities of her Necessitous and indigent Condition, upon the bettering thereof (by the general Ruine) raised in her such a quick sense of the misery of want, that she became most industriously provident, and resolvedly sparing and cautious for the future, and to prefer the certainty of her own care and diligence to the [externpore], fond and easie delusions of Deus providebit, *with which she had been fooled before into an almost voluntary and devoted poverty.*

This her Aspect and Consideration of the future, extended it self (with more prudence and sagacity then her Husband would descend to) in some humble thoughts of her present rise levelled to her past depression: She took a prophetical prospect of the Times, and having seen two, three or four variations in the calmnesse and tranquillity of her Husbands Fortunes, did wisely presage to her self that after those Hurly burlies of war and the Tempest of Rebellion, wherein he had whirled, and with so much impatient precipitancy engaged himself, there would another turn happen, against which she concluded to be more *discreetly Armed*. The first Eddy of that boysterous and unruly Current of his Prosperity, which at last over-ran all Banks and Boundaries flowed into the receptacle of her Committee-ship in the associated Counties, particularly *Cambridge* and *Huntingdon*, where to recover and peice[sic] up her ruines, she with the same Spirit of zeal and piety of her Husbands, consecrated her House to be the Temple of *Rapine*, one of the prime Goddesses next the *Cause*; whither for sacrifices all manner of Cattel clean and unclean, were brought from all the adjacent parts; as other costly utensils of the best moveables to adorn and enrich this sacred place; from whence to hope for any re-delivery was mental Sacriledge, and

Cameo pendant depicting Cromwell, set amongst rubies. Believed to have belonged to Elizabeth Cromwell.

to endevour[sic] it was punished with irreparable ruin; and I am sure (like the guilt of that crime) there are some who now feel it to the third generation, and may without miracle to perpetuity.

For not only was her Corban to be satisfied with the product of such oblations, but lands were to be set apart and sequestred[sic], the revenue of which past first through her fingers, and were made Impropriations of her own.

Having thus recruited her Estate, and adjusted her present Seizures to her past losses, and exalted above the Dignity of Mrs. Sheriff, or Countesse of those Shires, no person her equal in greatnesse; upon the Successe of her Husband after *Marston Moore* she abandoned the dull Country, partly not enduring the ordinary demeanor of her acquaintance towards her, nor sufferable nor endurable by her betters, for her imperious and unsociable Carriage towards all persons of quality; and partly to partake in the supreme fruition of the City's more elaborate & exquisite pleasures, & to huswife early admiration: for the Ladies of the Cause began to appear at Thanksgiving dinners, and to reckon as many dishes to a Messe, as their Husbands numbered atchievements.

At her Arrival in Town she was little lesse then saluted by the whole Juncto, though not in a body, yet severally by them all, and afterwards by the Pastours, Elders and Brethren of the Sects, who came not a House warming with the breath of their Mouths, in zealous gratulations, but brought all Silver Implements for her accommodation of housholdstuff, and offered them according to the late pattern of Reformation in *Guildhall*. Nor did tis humor cease here, the middle sort of the Religiously Phanatique, sent her in *Westphalia Hams, Neats Tongues, Puncheons,* and *Teirces* of *French Wine, Runlets,* and Bottle of Sack; all manner of Preserves and Comfits, to save her the trouble of the Town; the most of which gifts, they being multiplied upon her, she retailed by private hands, at as good a rate as the Market would afford.

But much more of these was given afterwards when *Oliver* was returned from the ending the war, and was lookt upon as the great Motion of the Parliaments proceedings: not to reckon on those immoderate Bribes that obtruded themselves upon her, more welcome by far then those Saintlike benevolences and civil Offices of Love, under which their corrupting practices were vailed to no purpose; for she very well understood the very first Addresses though never so innocently remote from the main design, and would rate them (as they do Post Miles, for she kept her constant distant Stages in all her publique brocage and Transactions) duely and exactly.

And indeed her House was in this respect a political or State *Exchange* by which the Affairs of the Kingdom were governed, and the prizes of all things set, whether Offices, preferments, Indempnity; as all other manner of Collusion and Deceipts were practised, and money stirring no where else: And in the other respect of *Provisions*, it might have pass'd for the Temple of *Bell* and the *Dragon*, (to persue the former Sanctity of her Rural Mansion) where all those offerings of Diet were consumed, or as good, altered and assimilated to her nature (the use of the nutritive faculty) by serving her Covetousnesse in their reduction to money.

Now she needed no such austere diligence in the preservation of an estate, for it was more than she and her Ministers could do to receive it. It was impossible to keep any Decorum or order, in that house where masterlesse money like a haunting Spirit, possessed and disquieted every room. It was a kind of *Midas* his Palace, where there was nothing but Gold to ear, only instead of being confined to that indigestible food, she and her Servants were most frequently invited out of Dores to most sumptuous and magnificent treatments, whence because of that more sacred employment at home, (like

Sabbatarians that provide themselves bak'd and cold meats for the superstitious observation of the day) they ant their progging Lady brought home such reliques, as they might mumble down in the dispatch of their businesse, and save the trouble or Magick of their long Graces, which had brought a Curse instead of a Blessing, upon their Masters and Mistresses first endevours, though she her self (so hard it is to forgoe and shake off an habitual customary Hypocrisie and falacy) would look as religiously upon a March pane, Preserve, or Comfit, as despairing Lover upon his Mistresses Lips.

But the War expired, and those Thanksgiving and triumphal Festivals over and ended, this pious family began to enter upon the years of Famine after those of Plenty. Her Husband was now engaged in deep designes and practices upon the King ad Kingdome, and in order to ruin them both, upon the Army; Every one of those mischievous and Matchiavilian Consultations and projects, were ushered continually by a Fast, which being appointed for, and observed by the Host, were always intimated to the friends and Relations of the Officers, and kept by them with no lesse strictnesse in their private Housholds; which by the frequent shifts, and various turns of policy, which *Cromwell*'s Fate, and the uncertainty of the Times guided him to, came so often and thick upon the neck of one another, that her Domesticks had almost forgot dinner time; upstart Piety, like the modern Frugality, baiting a Meal, and as that had limited the diet to Noon, this changed it and inverted it to night.

So that, as in other authoritative continued Fasts, there is a political and humane Reason, *viz.* the sparing the Creature, even to the same end, this good Huswife directed her domestick abstinence; and when on such occasions she had cause to suspect a general discontent of her people and household; she would up with this Scripture expression, and lay it in their Teeth for better fare; *The Kingdome of God is not Meat and Drink, but Righteousnesse and Peace,* and some such Scriptural dehortations from gluttony and the like luxurious Intemperance, and other zealous Sentences of Moderation in Diet; as that the pleasure of a full diet consists more in desire then in Satiety; that to have the Stomach twice repleated in the day, is to empty the Brain, and to render the mind unserviceable to the actions of life; No Abysse, no Whirlpool is so per[n]icious as Gluttony, which the more a man eats, makes him more a hungry,; and the better he dines to sup the worse, with such other Morals, taken out of *Gusman* and *Lazarillo de Tormes*, and only altered a little, by being made serious in practice.

Yet I cannot passe this necessary Lesson of Temperance, however it proceeds from this Sophistical corrupt Teacher thereof, without some reflection on some more ancient and authentique Instructions, but because it is a little beside my design, I will conclude them in some fit Sentences, as of the Satyrist *Persius*.

Poscis opem nervis Corpusque fidele Senectae,
Esto age sed grandes patinae tucetaque crassa
Annuere his superos vetuere Iovemque morantur.

Englished thus,
By *De Barten Holyday*.

Thou wishest for firm nerves, and for a sure Sound body, that would healthfully endure Until Old Age; why be it, that thy wish Is granted by the Gods; yet thy large Dish and full fat sasage make the Gods Delay To blesse thee, and do Force good Jove to stay.

And that other of *Epictetus*, worthy to be inscribed in all our parlours and Banquetting-Houses, [GREEK]. In another place *Inter Epulandum duos excipere debemus Convivas,* Corpus & Animam; *Tum quod in Corpus collatum sit repente effluxurum, quod autem in animam perpetuo servandum (i.e.)* in Feasting and banquetting we must except two Guests the body and the mind, because that which is bestowed on the body will suddenly passe away, and that which comes into the mind will be there laid up for ever; adding that commendation of *Plato* to a friend a Philosopher; *Vestrae quidem caenae non solum in praesentia sed etiam postero die sunt jucundae,* intimating that there is no such lasting pleasure as in a sober diet, which, when Excesses bring Surfeits, renews the Feast the next day, and gives a continual relish to the Appetite.

But I must beg pardon for this (otherwise seasonable) digression, and reduce the Discourse in pursuit of her Ladyships Errantry from one abode to another, in the suburbs of *London*, more or lesse like a Sojourner, (however she inhabited whole Houses) and a great person *incognito*, then as a Woman of that State and degree, to which her Husbands Condition and Command, and great probabilities of succeeding Titles, did forespeak her; If any thing could be observable by her for state and charge, it was the keeping of a Coach, the driver of which served her for Caterer, as much occasion as she had for him, for Butler, for Servingman, for Gentleman Usher, when she was to appear in any [publique] place. And this Coach was bought at the second hand, out of a great number, which then lay by the Walls, while their honourable owners went on foot, and ambled in the dirt to *Goldsmiths* and *Haberdashers-halls* if so fairly come by. She might, and she did ('twas thought) save that very inconsiderable Charge, but the sense she had how obvious and odious her Carriage in a sequestered Caroach would be to everybody, made her jealous of such scorn and derision; as for Horses she had them out of the Army, and their Stabeling and Livery in her husbands allotment out of the *Mews,* at the charge of the State; so that it was most thrifty and unexpensive pleasure and divertissement; (besides the finery and Honour of it) that could be imagined; for it saved many a meal at home, when upon pretence of businesse, Her Ladyship went abroad, and carrying some dainty povant for her own and her Daughters own repast, she spent whole days in short visits, and long Walks in the Ayre; so that she seemed to affect the *Scythian* fashion. Who dwell in Carts and Wagons, and have no other habitations.

Her publique Retinue was also very slender, and as slenderly accoutred, no more commonly, then one of her Husbands Horse boys running by her, sometimes one, and sometimes another; with or without Livery, all was one; on purpose (it may well be supposed, beside the saving the Cost) to prevent her being discryed and discovered, so much suspicion & hatred had her husband drawn upon himself, even from the vulgar which she feared, might by some such Badge of notice, light upon her self in the streets as she passed.

She was the same *recluse* likewise in her Habit, rather *harnessing* her self in the *defence* of her Cloaths, then allowing her self the loose and open bravery thereof, as not having been used to such *light armour*; and her Hood, till her face was seen in her Highnesses Glasse, was clapt on like a *Headpiece*, without the Art of *ensconcing* and *entrenching* it double in double and single *redoubts* and *hornworks*. In fine, she was *Cap a pe* like a *Baggage* Lady, and was out of her Element, in her vicinity to the Court and City.

But her Daughters were otherwise vested and robed, and a constant expence allowed in Tire-women, Perfumers, and the like Arts of Gallantry, , with each their Maid and Servant to attend them: and by their Array and Deportment, their quality might have been guessed at; they were all (those that were unmarried) very young: but Mrs. *Elizabeth*, who about this time was married to one Mr. *Claypole*'s Son of *Northamptonshire* (the old man having had a hand in the same disloyal Service with *Oliver*, in that county) but with a very private Wedding, no way suitable to that Port and Grandeur, which *Oliver* kept in the Army, where he was look'd upon with the same

Mrs Cromwell's Cookbook

Portrait of Elizabeth, the Cromwell's second daughter, circle of Peter Lely, c.1655. She married John Claypole, who Mrs Cromwell later lodged with after her husband and daughter's deaths in 1658.

reverence and respect as the General himself; all that was *Hymen* like in the celebration of it, was some freaks and pranks without the Aid and Company of a Fidler (which in those days was thought by their precise Parents to be altogether unlawful and favouring of Carnality, as the ring and form of Marriage, were thought superstitious and Antichristian) in *Nol*'s military rude way of spoyling of the Custard, and like *Jack Pudding*, throwing it upon one another, which was ended in the more manly Game of buffeting with Cushions, and flinging them up and down the room.

Neither appeared there the splendor and Ornament of Jewells, and Pearls, and the like Lusture of Gems, whose invidious refractions like poysonous Effluxes, might invenome the World with Spleen and Malice, at their plundered and stolen radiancy; for by the manifold Surrenders and Stormings of Housed and Castles, *Cromwell* had amassed good store of rarities, besides Meddals, and gold and silver Vessels (the spoyls of our Captivity) which it was not as yet safe to produce in such an unsettlement of his Conquest, till all propriety should be hudled up in the general ruine, out of whose mixt and confused rubbish, in his new polish'd Covernment, they might exert their Brightnesse underivable and clear from all former title and claim, as the Masse of things shall be meland calcined together, at the last universal Dissolution.

And I have heard it reported for a Truth, that most of rhe[*sic*] precious moveables, and other things of value, at the storming of *Basing house* by *Cromwell*, fell into his hands either immediately or directly, the Soldiers either by Command, or for some small price returning several precious pieces of rhe[*sic*] spoyle, whose worth they understood not, to his Agents, who gave an exact Account thereof to the Lady Reciever at home, who was about that time seen to be very pleasant and prajeant at the enjoyment of those pretty things (as she expres'd her self) being the best for substance and ornament, that belonged to the noble Marquiss of *Winchester* and his family, which this she-Usurper now lifted and Catalogued for her own.

And if the whole Inventory of her rapinous hoard were now producible, what a Voracious Monster would she appear to be? not[*sic*] a Corner in the Kingdome which is not sensible of her Ravage, and which had not a sharre in the Lombard of her uncountable and numberless Chattels.

How many rare pieces of antique Gold and Silver, are again damned to the earth from whence they were brought? and[*sic*] are by her mischievous Covetousnesse irrecoverably lost, which have been the glories and monumental pride of many Families? and[*sic*] only the remains and evidences of their noble Hospitality, now buried by this Wretch in hugger mugger.

Those advantages, together with the vails of the Army, which she had upon every Commission, and other incident occasions, for her Husbands Interests and Authority, together, with his Extraordinary pay, and the Apputunances to it, and Lands, and Hereditaments bestowed on Him, besides rewards and gratuities in ready money, amounted to an incredible Sum, which almost glutted her eyes to satiety, but so, that they were yet lesser than her belly, which could stow as much more with convenience enough, and conserve and secure it by a very parcimonious use, and narrow strict Disbursement; for having now quitted all Fears of returning to a private condition by the insolence of her Husbands Fortunes, which drove at the Soveraignty, the abhominable design being communicated to her; this great bank was still kept supplied by her, for the support and maintenance of that Dignity and Supremacy to which *Oliver* aspired, and to facilitate his way to it; having rightly perceived, that nothing but mony had carried on the War, and brought things to that passe, whatever was pretended of Zeal, and to the Cause, and therefore there was no difference in her manner of Housekeeping, only *Cromwell* being now in Town for the most part, conspiring that execrable Parricide against the King, she dispensed with her niggerly Regulation, and having taken a House neer *Charing-Crosse*, kept it in a manner open for all Comers, which were none but the *Sectary* party and Officers, who resorted thither as to their head-quarters, with all their wild projections, and were entertained with *Small Beer* and *Bread and Butter*, which to the animation of the approaching Villany, was as bad as *Aqua fortis* and *Horse Flesh*: for as was said of *Caesar, Nemo tm sobrius ad Rempublicam evertendam accessit, no man came more sober to the destruction of the Commonwealth*; so I may aptly and more justly say, That no men of more abstemiousnesse ever effected so vile and flagitious an enterprise upon so just a Government.

That being in perpetration, Mrs. *Cromwell* ran out of Purse some score of pounds (for it is to be remembered that she Stewarded it all along, *Oliver*'s head being busy with greater and worser matters) very much to her regret and vexation; but that Villany over; and some two or three private Treatments given his most sure and addicted Complices, in Exaltation of their monstrous Successe; the dores of the house were again barred, and all persons hindered, and of difficult admittance, upon what score or businesse soever; and now she was returned to her former privacy, and ordinary Diet as before.

During the rest of the time while *Cromwell* staid in *England*, she kept the same tenour, having received (besides a Confirmation of the Marquiss of *Worcester*'s Estate, to the value of *five thousand pounds* a year) upon the account of the defeat given the Levellers by her Husbands Treachery at a Thanksgiving dinner (where to he was invited by the City) a piece of Gold Plate of very good value, which discharged the former Expence.

I must omit many other passages during his absence in *Ireland* and in *Scotland*, and after this liminary, but prolix Account, sum up all in her menage of her Domestique Affairs at *Whitehall*, for which she had so long prepared and furnish her self with Rules of Government and Oeconomy, fitted for her Ursurpation and the Times.

For her Husband brought not so great and haughty, as she base and low spirited thoughts and resolutions to the grandeur of that place, the Habitation and Residence of the greatest and most famous Monarchs of the World, and famed throughout it for truly Royal and Princely Pomp, and immense Munificence and Entertainment.

She had flesh enough indeed to become any room in that spacious Mansion, but so little of a brave Spirit, that the least Hole of it would have made her a Banquetting House; but like a Spirit she came only to haunt, not to enjoy any part of it; The *Penates* and *Genii* of the place abhominating this prophane and sacrilegious Intrusion, neither giving him one hours quiet or rest in it, from his troubled,

View of the kitchen, Oliver Cromwell's House in Ely

mistrustful, and ill boding thoughts, nor her any Content and Satisfaction, but what she found in repining & vexing her self at the cost and Charge, the maintenance of that beggerly Court did every day put her to.

It was in the year 1653, that *Cromwell* first possessed and seated himself there, as in his own right, and in Chief, and brought his Worshipful Family thither, to their several apartments, she having appointed one Mr. *Maidstone* to be Steward of his House, and one Mr. *Starkey* to be his Master Cook (who afterwards was betrayed and taken drunk in his Cellar, designing the like upon my lord Maiors Sword-bearer, while my lord was in Conference with the Protector, so that he could not conceal it from the Household, who (out of spight to Him, as being a Spie over their Actions and behaviours) first acquainted their Lady, and she *Oliver* with the fault, aggravated by the Scandal and wastful Excesse; insomuch, that *Starkey* was commanded to come before him, where instead of a Complement and Excuse, He delivered himself by Vomit, in the very Face of his Master, and was thereupon dismissed the House.

It will not be too distant a Review to observe and remarque her Introduction to, and Seizin of this Royal Mansion, (which we have only mentioned) before any other procedure on the Oeconomy htereof.

The first Preparatory as to publique notice, was an Order from the new Conncil of State, after the dissolution of the parliament, commanding all persons to depart out of *White hall*, which was then the Den of a hundred several families, and persons of power, and office in the Anarchy; which being difficultly and grumblingly executed, she her self employed a Surveyor to make her some convenient accommodations, and little Labyrinths, and trap Stairs, by which she might at all times unseen, passe to and fro, and come unawares upon her Servants, and keep them vigilant in their places, and honest in the discharge thereof.

Several repaires were likewise made in her own appartments, and many small partitions up and down, aswel above Stairs, as in the Cellars and Kitchins, so that it looked like the Picture of *Bartholomew Faire;* Her Highnesship, not being yet accustomed to that roomy and August Dwelling, and perhaps afraid of the vastnesse and silentnesse thereof, which presented to her thoughts the Desolattion her Husband had caused, and the dreadful apparitions of those Princes, whose incensed Ghosts wandred up and down, and did attend some avenging opportunity; and this this was the more believable, because the (not to name her Husbands mis-giving Suspicions and frights) could never endure and Whispering, or to be alone by her self in any of the chambers.

And it is further here fit to be instanced, that upon her first coming, when her Harbingers had appointed her Lodgings, the same with the Queens, which yet retained their Royal Names and Distinctions, she would by no means hear of them but changed them into other Appellations, that there might remain no manner of disgust and discontent to her ambitious and usurping Greatnesse: and therefore they were adapted now into the like significations, by the name of the Protectors and Protectresses Lodgings, as more proper and fitter terms to their propriety, and indisputed possession.

Much adoe she had at first to raise her mind and deportment to this Soveraign Grandeur; and very difficult it was for her to lay aside those impertinent Meannesses of her private fortune; like the Bride-cat by *Venus's* favour metamorphosed into a comly Virgin, that could not forbear catching at mice, she could not comport with her present Condition, not forget the common converse and Affairs of Life; but like some Kitchin Maid preferred by the Lust of some rich and noble Dotard, was ashamed of her sudden and gawdy bravery, and for a while skulkt up and down the House, till the fawning observances and reverences of her Slaves had raised her to a Confidence, not long after sublimed into an impudence.

And this was helped on by Madam *Pride*, and my Ladies *Hewson*, and *Eerkstead, Goff, Whalley*, &c. [etc.] who all came to Complement her Highnesse upon the Felicity of *Cromwell's* Assumption to the Government, and to congratulate her Fortune, and so accompany her to her Palace of *Whitehall*, where like the Devil *cast out*, she *entered* by *Fasting* and *Prayer*, after the usual manner, and like devout *Jezabel*, took possession of *Naboth's* Vineyard.

And thus we have waited on her to this *Basilicon*, now swept and cleaned for her *friendly* entertainment; and the Chymneys smoked and heated again, which had suffered so long a *damp*; and after so long a Vacation; Especially her Highnesse took care, and gave strict charge to have all the rooms *aired*, for fear of those ill Sents the *Rump* had left behind them and was willing to be at the charge of Perfumes to expel the noysomnesse thereof, the account of which hath been seen by divers, allowed by her own hand; but foul odour was so equally natural to all the Grandees, that *Oliver* when he died left it in a worse condition then when he found it, as is publique in several Treatises.

Cromwell was now his own Steward and Carver, not limited to any expenses of Housekeeping, no more then to the Charges of the Government; but was absolute both at Dinner and at Council Board, neither of which were yet well serled; And therefore, besides the nearness of his Wife, it was necessary he should appear extraordinary frugal pf the peoples Purse, (who wish'd every bit he eat might choke him, for all his temperance) in his private and publique Disbursements. Only that he might not appear so much a Military Governor, but have something of the Prince in him, about Noon time, a man might hear a huge clattering of Dishes, and noise of

Servitors, in rank and file marching to his Table (though neither sumptuously nor extraordinarily furnished) in some imitation of *Paulus Aemilius* in his answer to the *Grecians*, after his Triumph and Conquest or *Perseus*, the last *Macedon* King; *Ejusdem effe Animi & Aciem & Convivium instrueere, illam quidem ut formidolosus Hostibus hoc ut Amicis gratus appareat*; in English thus, *'Tis of the same spirit to order a Battle, as to furnish a Feast, by the one a man appears terrible to his enemies, and by the other pleasing to his Friends.*

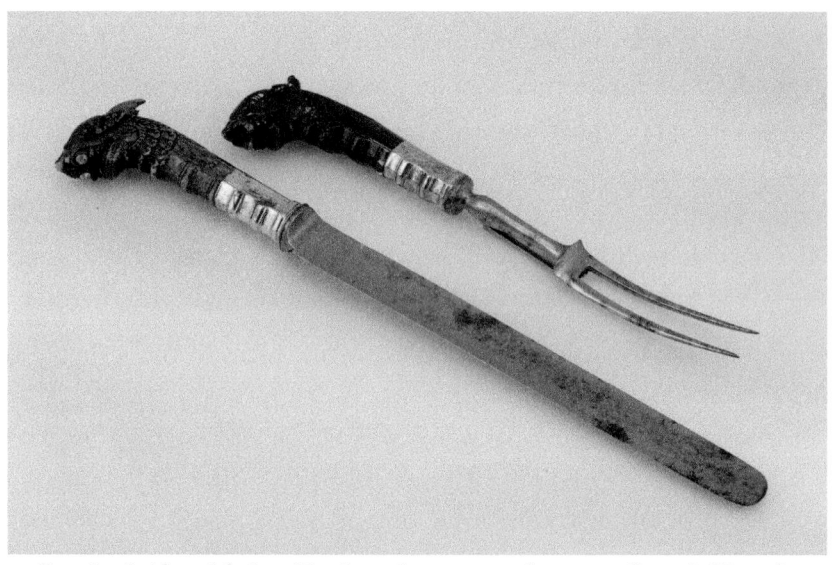

Carving knife and fork, said to have been captured amongst discarded Royalist baggage at the Battle of Naseby, 1645.

But at his private Table, very rarely or never, were our *French quelque-choses*, suffered by him or any such modern *Gusto's*, whether with the Fright he was prejudiced of Poyson, by such devices, (at an vitation made him and his General the Lord *Fairfax*, with the other of the supreme Commanders of the Army, by a small Officer therein, who was formerly a Cook) at a Ladies in *Hammersmith*, where with one Leg of Mutton drest all sorts of ways he entertained them all, but upon their discovery of the Fellowes audaciousnesse in bidding them, which prompted them to believe it was a design against their lives, and put most of them to the Vomit, was like to have been drest himself by the Hangman) or by stronger or more Masculine Appetite, which partaked with his other robust faculties, is uncertain; sure it is, that when in Treatments given his Familiars, such things were set upon the Table, 'twas more for shew and sport then for Belly Timber, and about which the good Huswife never troubled her head.

She, to return to her Government, very providentially kept two or three Cowes in St. *James's* Park, and erected a new Office of a Dairy in *Whitehall*, with Dairy Maids to intend that businesse solely, (as most of the Employment for Servants was managed by Females, for there were no Sergeants but such as waited with Halbeirds on the Guard) and fel to the old Trade of cherming Butter, and making Buttermilk, nor were *Oxford Kates* fine things, half so famous among the Cavalier Ladies, as my Lady Protectors Butter among the Mushrome zealous Ladies of the Court, most whereof, being Apple, or Oyster-women, or Stocking-Heelers, and the like, did much wonder at, and magnifie the invention and rarity.

Next to this Coy of Milk Maids she had another of Spinsters, and Sowers, to the number of six, who sate the most part of the day, after she was ready, in her privy Chamber sowing and stitching; they were all of them Ministers Daughters, such as were inveterate Nonconformists to the Church, for which cause, and the pretence of piety (the main ingredient to things of the least Moment) they were added to the Family; Nor did the Turkish Ministers take more care to furnish the *Seraglio*, and gratifie their Master with choice Virginities, then some of these pious Pimps did lay out for indigent godly Maidens to pleasure this prostitute Charity of hers, that the world might take notice of her exemplary Humility and compassion. But indeed all persons of breeding and quality, abhorred the indignity of her Service, and so rather than be served with common Drudges, she erected this new order, and continued it to the term of her Usurpation. Herein following the Steps of her Husband, who made a new daring Militia of zealous persons, since he could not be served with generous Spirits.

She was once resolved by the Assistance and Advice of her Mother, to have made a small brewing place, with Vessels, and other accommodation for her own, and *Oliver*'s Drink, as not liking the City Brewing, nor trusting to the Artifices of the Town; but about the same time a Drink was then grown famous in *London*, being a very small Ale of 7s. 6d. a Barrel, well boyled, and well tasted and conditioned, called, and known by the name of *Morning Dew* (From the Brewers name as I have heard) which was thence brought into request at Court, and was the Diet Drink of this temperate Couple, and the cool refreshing entertainment of those bouncing Ladies that came weltring and wallowing in their Coaches instead of Drayes to visit Her.

And for the Kitchin and Pantry a great Reformation was intended, but the multitude of Comers and Goers upon her first setling there, and number of Mouths which came gaping for preferment, being to be stopt with Victuals, put her besides her proposed Regulation, yet was there not a joynt of Meat for which the Cook was not to give an account, which she overlook'd, as it came from them to the Steward, whose accounts likewise were punctually cast up by her, and firmed by her hand, aswell as afterwards by the Protectors.

Nay, so severe and strict she was in this thrifty way of House-keeping, that she descended to the smallest and meanest matters, the very Chaffer, and price of the Market, and that the Reader may not think he is imposed on and deceived by a general imputation f her niggadlynesse; I will give him two notable and apposite instances.

The first, was the very next Summer after his coming to the Protectorate in 1654. in *June*, at the very first season of Green Pease, where a poor Country Woman living somewhere about *London*, having a very early but small quantity in her Garden, was advised to gather them and carry them to the Lady Protectoresse, her Counsellors conceiving she would be very liberal in her reward, they being the first of that year; accordingly the poor Woman came to the *Strand*; and having her Pease amounting to a Peck and a half, in a Basket, a Cook by the *Savoy* as she passed, either seeing or guessing at them, demanded the Price, and upon her silence offered her an Angel for them, but the Woman expecting some greater matter, went on in her way to *Whitehall*, where after much adoe, she was directed to her Chamber, and one of her Maids came out, and understanding it was a Present and Rarity, carried it in to the Protectresse, who out of her Princely Munificence cent her a Crown, which the Maid told into her hand; The Woman seeing this basenesse, and the frustration of her hopes, and remembring withal what the Cook had proffered her; *threw back the money into the Maids hands, and desired her to fetch back her Pease, for that she was offered five shillings more for them before she brought them thither, and could go fetch it presently*; and so half flightingly and half ashamedly, this great Lady returned her present putting it off with a censure upon the unsatisfactory daintinesse of luxurious and prodigal Epicurisme: the very same Pease were afterwards sold by the Woman to the said Cook, who is yet alive to justifie the truth of this Relation.

The other is of a later date, upon *Oliver*'s Rupture with the *Spanyard*, the Commodities of that Country grew very scarce, and the prizes of them raised by such as could procure them underhand: Among the rest of those goods, the fruits of the growth of that place were very rare and dear, especially *Oranges* and *Lemons*.

One day, as the Protector was private at dinner; He called for an *Orange* to a Loyne of Veal, to which he used no other Sauce, and urging the same command, was answered by his Wife, *that Oranges were Oranges now, that Crab Oranges would cost a Groat, and for her part, she never intended to give it*; and it was presently whispered, that sure her Highness was never the adviser of the *Spanish* War, and that his Highness should have done well to have consulted his Digestion, before his hasty and inordinate appetite of Dominion and Riches in the *West Indies*.

I might confirm this by other retrenchments of Expence, whensoever she could confine his Table to her own privacy; particularly it was a great Mode, and taken up by his Court party to roast half Capons, pretending a more exquisite tast and nutriment in it, then when dressed whole and entire; where I cannot but smile to think how it puzzled her Ladyships Carver, to hold him to the knife, and to apportion half and quarter Limbs according to Art. Much more do I wonder what those Fellows at *Rome* did, or what they would have done here, who kept carving Schools *ludi structorii*, and had all manner of Fowl and Fish, and such other grand Festival meat carved in Wood, which they marked out with wooden Knives with very great curiosity, and instructed their Scholars, who learned it as a worshipful Employment and a way to preferment, as the Satyrist very elegantly.

Sumine cum magno lepus atque aper & Pygargus,
Et Scythicae volucres, & Phenicopterus ingens,
Et Getulus Oryx hebeti lautissima Ferro
Caeditur, & tota sonat ulmea caena suburra.

Englished thus,
The Sow's large Teat, the Hare and Bore and Deer,
Scythian, & Africks Fowl and Bearded Beast,
The Gawdies of the Town, in Wood appear,
So with dull Iron carv'd sounds Elmy Feast.

And if it were not made almost incredible by the Superfluity and excesse of her fortune, which cannot be supposed to have no way advanced her thoughts from her former industry, and frugal care and intendency.

I might insert a story of her enquiry into the profit of the Kitchin-stuff, and the exchanging of it for Candles, which those that knew her humour had purposely put into her head; till she was told to whom it belonged; and the Customes of the Court, to most of which she answered, they should not think to have them take place as in the *other Womans days*, for she would look better to it: like *Vespasian*, she had learnt, That *Dulcis odor lucre ex re qualibet*, Gain was sweet from what ever thing.

And the reason she used to give for this her frugal Inspection and Parcimony, was the small allowance and mean pittance she had to defray the Houshold Expences, which at her first coming to Court keeping, was barely sixty four thousand pounds *per annuum*, until Collonel *Philip Jones*, came to be Comptroller of the household, when the weekly charge was Nineteen hundred twenty three pounds odd money, the defalcation of the rest, from the just sum of two thousand pounds, at the rate of a 100000 *l.* yearly, making up the four thousand pound for the two Weeks, above the 50. so exactly was this charge computed, and method punctually observed, that there might be no place for Excesse, and by means thereof, for deceit or any colluding practises.

Her order of Eating and Meal times, was not lesse regulated, and though inverted, yet designed well to the decency aswell as conveniency of her Service; for first of all, a t the ringing of a Bell dined the Halberdiers, or men of the Guard with the inferiour Officers; then the Bell rung again, and the Stewards Table was set (in the same Hall neer the Water Stairs) for the better sort of those that waited on their Highnesses; Ten of whom were apportioned to a Table or Messe, one of which was chosen by themselves every week for Steward, and he gave the Clerk of the Kitchin the Bill of Fare, as was agreed upon generally every morning: to these Ten men, and what Friends should casually come to visit them, the value of 10. shillings in what flesh or fish soever they would have, with a Bottle of Sack, & two of Claret, was appointed; but to prevent afterComers from expecting any thing in the Kitchin, there was a general rule, that if any man thought his businesse would detain him beyond dinner time, he was to give notice to the Steward of his Messe, who would set aside for him as much as his share came too, and leave it in the Buttery.

Suppers likewise they had none, Eggs or some slaps contenting *Cromwell* and her Ladyship; and to his Exemplar all was conformed; in lieu thereof, for the Family there was constantly boyled 8 Stone of Beef early in the morning, to keep her Retainers in heart and earnest of a dinner, the Broth thereof, and all the Scraps and Reliques of dinner, (to give her her due) were alternately given to the Poor of

17th century woodcut of a family dining.

Saint *Margarets Westminster*, and Saint *Martins* in the Fields, according to the Churchwardens Roll of each Parish, and that very orderly, without any Brabble or noise; so that amidst so many Curses and imeprecations, which were uttered against him; he had some Prayers and Blessings from those hungry *Jack Dawes*, that frequented and attended this *Dole*. But those lame, decrepit, and starved precepts, never reached half way, and like impotent suspended Meteors, hoysed half Region high, fell distinctly at last upon himself and Family.

His Feasts was none of the liberallest, and far from magnificence even those two he gave the *French* Embassador, and the Parliament in 1656, upon their gratulation of his *Syndercombe* deliverance, which last amounted not to above 1000 *l.* and she saved 200 *l.* of it in the Banquet, for a Big Bellied Woman, a Spectator, neer *Cromwell's* Table, upon the serving thereof with Sweatmeats; desiring a few dried Candies of Apricocks, Col. *Pride* sitting at the same, instantly threw into her Apron a Conserve of Wet, with both his hands, and stained it all over; when as if that had been the Sign, *Oliver* catches up his Napkin and throwes it at *Pride*, he at him again, while all of that Table were engaged in the Scuffle: the noise whereof made the Members rise before the Sweat-meats were set down, and believing dinner was done, goe to this pastime of Gambols, and be Spectators of his Highnesses Frolicks. Were it worth a Description, I could give the Reader a just and particular account of that *Ahab* Festival, as it was solemnized in the Banquetting House of *Whitehall*.

But I must passe it, and those other Nuptial Entertainments at the Marriage of his Daughters, and the Treats he gave to Duke *De Crequi*, and Monsieur *Mancin* the Cardinal's great Counsellors, and Familiars Nephew, as things beyond her Sphere, and out of her charge and my purpose, and instance the common ordinary diet of this Family, whereby the Reader will better perceive, and be perhaps advantaged also by the intention and nature of this Discourse.

Here followes the most usual Meat and Diet observed at her Table, most of them ordinary and vulgar, except some few Rarities, but such as arrided her Palate and Expence, of which it will be no unpleasing Labour to the Reader, to peruse the *Cookery*, and manner of Dressing, as also her Preserves, &c.

The Recipes

***How* to make a *Rare* Dutch *Pudding*.**
Take a pound and a half of *fresh* Beef, all lean, take a pound and a quarter of Beef Suet, sliced both very small, then take a half penny stale Loaf and grate it, a handful of Sage, and a little Winter Savory, a little Time, shred these very small; take four Eggs, half a pint of Cream, a few Cloves, *Nutmegs*, Mace and Pepper finely beaten, mingle them altogether very well, with a little Salt; roll it all up together in a green Colwort Leaf, and then tye it up hard in a Linnen Cloth, garnish your Dish with grated bread, and serve it up with Mustard in Sawcers.

***How* to roast a *Leg of Mutton the French way*.**
Take half a pound of Mutton and a quarter of a pound of Suet, season it with sweet Hearbs, and a little Nutmeg, and two or three Shallots; slice these very small, and stuff the Mutton round, then take some of the best *Hackney* Turnips, and boyl them in Beef Broth very tender, then squeeze the water from them a little, set them in a Dish under the Leg of Mutton when it is half roasted and so let the gravy drop into them, and when the meat is roasted serve them in a Dish with it, with a little Fresh Butter and Vinegar, garnish your Dish with sliced Onions and Parsley, and some of the Turnip sliced.

***How* to make Scotch collops of Veal**. **(this was almost Her constant Dish.)**
Take a Fillet of Veal, cut it out into very broad slices, fat and lean, not too thick; take eight Eggs, beat them very well with a little salt, grate a whole Nutmeg, take a handful of Thyme and strip it, take a pound of Sawsedges, half a pint of Stewing Oysters, the largest to be

had, wash and cleanse them from the Gravel: then half fry your Veal with sweet Butter, then put in your Sawsedges and Oysters, then take a quarter of a pound of Capers, shred them very small; three Anchovis, dissolve them in white Wine and fair water, so put in your Eggs, shred Capers, and Anchovis, Butter and Spice, and mingle them, and strew them in the Pan upon the Veal and Oysters; serve it with Sippets, with a little fresh butter, and vinegar, and Limons sliced, and Barberies, with a little salt. You must have a care to keep the meat stirring, lest the Eggs curdle with the heat of the fire.

How to souse a Pig and collar it like a Brawn.
After you have stuck the pig let him bleed well, then with scalding water and Rozin finely beaten take off the Hair, let him lye in cold water a little space, shifted two or three times, that he may look white, then cut off the Feet, slit him open, and take out his inwards, and cut off his head, take the two sides asunder, lay them in cold water, steep it there a day and night, shifting the water thrice, then take out the bones; roll up each side several, tying them as hard as possible, in the fashion of a Collar of Brawn, then tye it up in a Cloth hard, and put the head whole in another, then boyle it in water and Salt, Cloves, Mace and Nutmeg, and a handful of *Rosemary*, and some Sweet herbs, while it is very tender; take it up and let it cool, then put it into the liquor that boyled it, adding thereto two quarts of Small beer; set the two Collars in a Dish garnished with Salt, (with the head entire in the middle) and stick in two Sprigs of Rosemary flowred, and serve it with Sawcers of Mustard.

How to make a Sweet Pye with Lamb-stones, and Sweet-breads, and Sugar.
Take the Lambstones and slit them in the middle, and skin them, wash the Sweatbreads both of Veal and Lamb, and wipe them very drye, take the Lambs Liver and shred it very small; take the Udder

of a Leg of Veal and slice with it, season all with a little salt, Nutmeg, Mace, and Cloves beaten, and two whole Pepper, then shred two or three Pippins and candid Limon and Orange peel, half a dozen dates sliced, with Currants and White Sugar, a few Carroway seeds, a quarter of a pint of Verjuice, and as much Rosewater; a couple of Eggs; Roll up all these together in little puddings or Balls made green with the juice of Spinnage, and lay a pudding, then a Sweatbread, and then a Lambstone, till you have filled up the Pye, and cover them with Dates and sliced Citron and Limon. When it is drawn take two or three Yelks of Eggs, beat them, and put then to a little fresh Butter, White wine, and Sugar, and pour it into the Tunnel, scrape some Loaf Sugar upon the Lid and so serve it.

A rare **White-pot.**
Take three pints of Cream, whole Cinamon, a [little] sliced Nutmeg, set on the Cream, and spice and scall'd it, take a penny Loaf, slice it very thin, take a Couple of Marrow-bones, lay the Marrow sliced on the bottome of the Dish, upon the Marrow lay the bread, then lay Raisins of the Sun over the bread, and lay Marrow again as before, to the 3-pints of scalded cream add 9 Yelks of Eggs well beaten, with Rose-water, sweeten the cream with white Sugar, and take ont the whole Cinamon, and beat he Cream and eggs well, fill up a broad shallow Basin, and bake it; when 'tis enough scrape fine Sugar on it, and stick it with red and white Muskadoes, and so serve it.

A rare **Citron *Pudding*.**
Take a penny Loafe and grate it, a pint and a half of Cream, half a dozen of eggs, one Nutmeg sliced, a little Salt, an Ounce of candied Citron sliced small, a little candied Orange Peel sliced, 3 Ouncesof Sugar, put those into a wooden Dish well flowered and covered with a Cloth, and when the water boyleth put it in; boyl it well, and serve it up with Rose-water and stick it with Wafers or blanch'd Almonds.

Mrs Cromwell's Cookbook

How to make Liver Puddings.

Take the Guts of a young Hog, wash them very clean, and lay then two or three days in the water, take the Liver of the same Hog and boyle it till it will grate, then grate it very small and fine, take to the weight of the Liver almost the weight of Beef Suet, season it with Salt, Cloves, Mace and Nutmeg, finely beaten, a penny Loaf grated, a pound of the best white Sugar, two pound of good Currants, a pint of good Cream a quarter of a pint of Rose water, three eggs; mixe altogether to such a thicknesse as you may fill the Guts, then prick them, and put them into boyling water, and keep an even fire for half a quarter of an hour, then take them up and lay them upon straw; you must have a care in boyling them, [that] you tye them not too hard nor too slack, lest they break.

How to make Marrow Puddings, **(which she usually had to her breakfast.)**

Take a pound of the best Jordan Almonds, blanch them, beat them fine in a stone or wooden Mortar (not in brasse) with a little Rose-water, take apound of fine powder Sugar, a penny Loaf grated, grated Nutmeg, a pint of Cream, the Marrow of two Marrow-bones, two grains of Ambergris; mingle them altogether with a little Salt, fill the skins, boyl them gently as before.

How to make Marrow Pasties.

Take some Marrow and Apples, sherd the Marrow and Apples, and put tot hem a little Sugar; put them into puff past, and frie them in a pan with fresh butter, and serve them up to the table with a little white sugar strowed in it.

A Country way to make Sawsedges.

Take Pork, not so much fat as lean, mince it exceeding small together, then take part of the Fleck of Pork, which is the Suet, in pieces about the bignesse of the top of your finger, season each apart with minced Sage, good store of Pepper and Salt, some cloves and Mace, mix in the seasoning into each of them; take the small sheeps Guts, and cleanse them, (others use Capons Guts) and fill them with your Funnel, always putting some of the Fleck between the minced, if you have it ready you may sprinckle a little Sack on the top of the Sawsedge Meat, it will make it fill the better.

Another way.
Cut a Gammon that is very red; and half boyl it, mince it very small, if the Gammon be not fat, take half as much Lard of Bacon, mince it likewise, mingle them together, and beat them in a Mortar, season it with Time and Sage minced very small, and good store of Pepper beaten to dust, with a little Clover, Mace; and Nutmeg, and a pretty quantity of Salt, for they must tast of that very strong, add to them the Yolk of two Eggs, and so much red wine as will bring them up into a stiff body, mingle them well with your hands, fill them into middle Skins as big as ordinary Sawsedges, then hang them in the Cymney for a time, they are not to be eaten in the Skin, but must be cut out very thin roundways, and do serve for Sallet all the year long.

To make green Sawce.
Take a handful, or a greater quantity of Sorrel, beat it in a Mortar with Pippins pared and quartered, add thereto a little Vinegar and Sugar, put it into Sawcers. Otherwise take Sorrel, best it and stamp it well in a Mortar, scruze out the juice of it, put thereto a little Vinegar, Sugar, and two hard eggs minced small, a little Butter and grated Nutmeg, set this upon the Coals till it is hot, and pour it into the dish on the Sippets, this is Sawce for Hen or Veal or Bacon.

To dresse Udders and Tongues.

When they are boyled enough in the Beef Pot and skinn'd, you must have your Turnips ready boyled, cut in peices and soakt in Butter, or otherwise Collyflowers and Carrets, or all of them, then put the Turnips all over the bottom of a large dish, then slice out the Tongues and lay the sides one against another, garnish the Collyflowers all over them, and the Carrets up and down between the Collyflowers, with Barberies and Parsley in the brim of the dish.

To make Goosberry Cream.

First boyle, or you may preserve your Goosberries, then having a clear Cream boyled up and seasoned with old Cinamon, Nutmeg, Mace, Sugar, Rose-water and Eggs, dish it up, and when it is cold take up the Goosberries with a pin, and stick them on in rounds aas thick as they can lye upon the said Cream, garnishing your Dish with them, and strow them over with the finest Sugar and sever them up.

To make Punnado.

Take one quart of running water, put it on the fire in a Skillet, then cut a light Roul of bread in slices, about the bignesse of a groat, and as thin as Wafers, lay it on a dish on a few Coals, then put it into the water with two handful of Currants, pickt and washt, a little large Mace, season it with Sugar and Rosewater, when it is enough.

To make a Sack Posset.

Set a Gallon of Milk on the fire, put therein whole Cinnamon and large Mace, when it boyls stir in a half or whole pound of Naples bisket grated very small, keeping of it stirring while it boyls, then beat 8 Eggs together, casting of the whites away, beat them well with a Ladleful of Milk, then take the Milk off the Fire and stir in the eggs, then put it on again, but keep It stirring for fear of curdling, then make ready a pint of Sack, warming it upon Coals with a little

Rose-water; season your Milk with Sugar, and pour it into the Sack in a large basin, and stir it apace, then strow on a good deal of beaten Cinnamon, and so serve it up.

To make a Dish of Apples.

Put on a Skillet of water with some Currants a boyling; then pare about a dozen Pippins, and cut them from the Core into the said water, when they are boyled tender, pour them into a Cullendar, when the [water] is drained from them, put them into a dish and season them (but if you have time stay until they are cold, let it melt your sugar, besides it will spoil the Tast) with Sugar, Rose-water, Cinnamon, and Carraway-seeds, then roll out two sheets of past; put one in the Dish bottome, and all over the Brims, then lay in the Apples in the bottom round and high, wet it round and cover it with he other sheet; close it and carve it about the brims of the Dish as you please, prick it and bake it, scrape Sugar upon it and serve it up.

To roast Eels.

When they are slead, cut them to peices about three or four inches long, drye them, and put them into a Dish, mince a little Time, two Onions, a peice of Lemmo Pill, a little Pepper beaten small, Nutmeg, Mace and Salt, when it is cut exceeding small, strow it on the Eels with the Yolk of two or three Eggs, then having a small Spit (otherwise a couple of square sticks made for that purpose) spit through the Eele cross ways, and put a bay Leaf between every peice of Eele, and tying the sticks on a Spit let them roast. You need not turn them constantly, but let them stand until they hisse, or are brown, so do them on the other side, and put the dish (in which the Eele was with the seasoning) underneath to save the gravy, bast it over with sweet Butter. The sawce must be a little Claret Wine, some minced Oysters with their liquor, a grated Nutmeg and an Onion, with sweet Butter, and so serve it.

Preparing Eels in the kitchen at Oliver Cromwell's House, Ely

To make an Eele Pye.

Your Eels being flead, washed, and cut in pieces, as long as you think convenient, put to them a handful of sweet herbs, Parsley mixed with Onion, season them with Pepper, Salt, Cloves, Mace, and Nutmeg, and having your Coffin made of good past, put them in and strew over them, two handful of Currants, and a Limon cut in slices, then put on Butter and close the Pye, when it is baked, put in at the Funnel a little sweet Butter, white Wine and Vinegar, beaten up with a couple of Yolks of Eggs.

To dresse a **Cods** *head.*

Cut off the Codds head beyond the Gills, that you may have part of the body with it, boyl it in water [and] salt, to which you may add half a pint of Vinegar, the head must be a little more then covered before you put it in the Caldron, take a quart of the biggest cleanest oysters, and a bunch of sweet herbs and Onions, and put them into the mouth of the head, and with a packthread behind the Jawes saft, you must be sure to prick it and wash it very clean, when it is Boyled enough, take it up and set it a drying over a Chafingdish of Coals, then take the Oyster Liquor, four Anchoves, and a sliced Onion; put to them a quarter of a pint of white Wine, and sweet butter, and melt them together, and pour it on the Cods head, stick all or most of the Oysters upon the head, or where they will enter, and garnish it over with them, grate on a little Nutmeg, and send it smoking up, garnish the brims of the dish with Limon and sliced bay Leaves.

To boyle Perches.

Let your Liquor boyle, and your Pan be seasoned with a little white Wine, a couple of Onions cut in halfs, and a bunch of sweet hearbs, and a little white Pepper, boyl them up very quick, and flea them on both sides, and dish them upon Sippets, then take a little white Wine, gravy, and Vinegar, with a grated Nutmeg, and almost boyl it over a Chafing-dish, then pour sweet Butter over it; garnish it with Barberies and sliced Limmons.

To boyle Eeles.

Cut the Eeles as before, and stew them, when they are half done, beat a little Ale with Vinegar, and put into the Liquor, with some Parsley and sweet hearbs: Dish them and serve them up in their broth with a little Salt.

To boyle Woodcocks or Snipes.

Boil them either in strong broth, or in water and salt, and bein boyled take out the Guts and chop them small with the Liver, put it to some crumbs of grated whitebread, a little of the Broth of the Cock, and some large Mace; stew them together with some gravy, then dissolve the yolks of two Eggs with some wine Vinegar, and a little grated Nutmeg, and when you are ready to dish it, put the eggs to it, and stir it amongst the sauce with a little Butter; dish them on sippets, and run the sauce over them with some beaten Butter, and Capers, or lemon minced small, barberries or whole pickled grapes.

Sometimes with this sauce boile som slic'd onions, and currans boil'd in a broth by itself; when you boil it with onions rub the bottome of the dish with Garlick.

How to boil Cocks or Larks otherwayes.
Boil them with the Guts in them, in strong broth, or fair water, and three or four whole onions, large mace, and salt; the Cocks being boil'd, make sauce with some thin slices of Manchet or grated bread in another Pipkin, and some of the broth where the fowl or the cocks boile, then put to it some butter and the guts and liver minced, then have some yolks of eggs dissolved with some Vinegar, and some grated nutmeg, put it to the other ingredients, stir them together, and dish the fowl on fine sippets, pour on the sauce with some slic't lemon, grapes, or barberries, and run it over with beaten butter.

To boile Capons, Pullets, Chickens, Pigeons, Pheasants or Partridges.
Fearce then either with the bone or boned, then take off the skin whole, wit the legs, wings, neck, and head on, mince the body with some bacon or beef-suet, season it with nutmeg, pepper, cloves, beaten ginger, salt and a few sweet herbs finely minced and mingled among some 3 or 4 yolks of eggs, some sugar, whole grapes, gooseberries, barberries, and pitaches; fill the skins and prick them up in the back, then stew them between two dished with some strong broth, white wine, butter, some large Mace, marrow, gooseberries, and sweet herbs; being stew'd serve them on sippets with some marrow and slic'd lemon; in winter, currans.

To boil a Chicken or Capon in White Broth.

First boyl the Capon in water and salt, then take three pints of strong broth, white wine, and stew it in a pipkin with a quarter of a pound of dates, half a pound of dates, half a pound of fine sugar, four or five blades of large mace, the marrow of 3 marrow bones, a handful of white endive; stew these in a pipkin very leisurely, that it may only simper, then being finely stew'd and the broth well tasted, strain the yolks of ten eggs with some of the broth, before you dish up the Capons or Chickens, put in the eggs int the broth, and keep it stirring that it may not curdle, give it a walm and set it from the fire; the fowls being dished up put on the broth, and garnish the meat with dates, marrow, large mace, endive, preserved barberies, and oranges, boil'd skirrets, poungarnet, curnells. Make a lear of almond paste and grape verjuyce.

A Turkish dish of meat.

Take an interlarded piece of Beef, cut it into thin slices, and put it into a pot that hath a close cover, or stewing pan; then put into it a good quantity of clean picked rice, skin it very well, and put into it a quantity of whole pepper, two or three whole onions, and let this boile very well, then take out the onions, and dish it on sippets, the thicker it is the better.

To stew a Fillet of Beef in the Italian Fashion.

Take a young tender fillet of beef, and take away all the skins and sinews clean from it, put to it some good white wine (that is not too sweet) in a boul, wash it and crush it well in the wine, then strow upon it a little pepper, and a poulder called *Tamara* in *Italian*, and as much salt as will season it, mingle them very well, and put to it as much white wine as will cover it, lay a trencher upon it to keep it down I a close pan with a weight on it, and let it steep two nights and a day; then take it out and put it into a pipkin with some good beef broth, but put none of the pickle to it, but onely beef broth: and that sweet, not salt; cover it close, and set it on the embers, then put to it a few whole cloves and mace, and let it stew till it be enough, it will be very tender and of an excellent taste; serve it with the same broth as much as will cover it.

To make this *Tamara*, take two ounces of coriander seed, an ounce of aniseed, an ounce of fennel seed, two ounces of cloves, and an ounce of cinamon; beat them into a gross powder, with a little powder of winter savory, and put them into a viol glass to keep.

To make an excellent Pottage called Skinke.

Take a leg of beef, and chop it into three peices, then boil it in a pot with three pottles of spring water, a few cloves, mace, and whole pepper; after the pot is scummed, put in a budle of sweet marjoram, rosemary, time wintersavory[sic], sage and parsley, bound up hard, some salt, and two or three great onions whole; then about an hour before dinner put in three marrow bones, and thicken it with some stained oatmeal, or manchet slic't and steeped with some gravy, strong broth, or some of the pottage: then a little before you dish up the Skinke, put into it a little fine poulder of Saffron, and give it a walm or two; dish it on large slices of French Bread, and dish the marrow-bones on them in a fine clean large dish; then have two or three manchets cut into toasts, and being finely toasted, lay on the knuckle of beef in the middle of the dish, the marrow bones round about it, and the toasts round about the dish brim, serve it hot.

To stew a Rump or the fat end of a Brisket of Beef in the French fashion.

Take a Rump of Beef, boil it and scum it clean, in a stewing pan or broad mouthed pipkin, cover it close and let it stew an hour; then put to it some whole pepper, cloves, mace, and salt, scotch the meat with your Knife to let out the gravy, then put in some Clarret wine, and half a dozen of scic'd Onions; having boil'd, and hour after put in some Capers, or a handful of brome buds, and half a dozen of Cabbidge-lettice being first parboil'd in fair water, and quartered, two or three spoonfuls of wine vinegar, and as much verjuice, and let it stew till it be tender; then serve it on sippets of French bread, and dishit on those sippets; blow off the fat clean off the Broth, or scum it, and stick it with fried bread.

To boil a Chine, Rump, Surloine, Brisket, Rib, Flank, Buttock, or Fillet of Beef powdered.

Take any of these, and give them in summer a weeks powdering, in winter a fortnight, stuff them or plain; if you stuff them, do it with all manner of sweet herbs, fat beef minced, and some nutmeg; serve them on brewis, with roots or cabbidge boil'd in milk, with beaten Butter, &c.

To pickleroast Beef, Chine, Surloine, Rib, Brisket, Flank, or Neats Tongues.

Take any of the foresaid Beef, as chine or fore-rib, and stuff it with pennyroyal, or other sweet herbs, or parsley minced small, and some salt, prick in here and there a few whole cloves, and rost it; then take Claret wine, wine vinegar, whole pepper, rosemary, and bayes, and time bound up close in a bundle, and boil'd in some Claret wine, and wine vinegar, make the pickle, and put some salt to it, then pack it up close in a Barrel that will but just hold it, put the pickle to it, close it on the head, and keep it for your use.

To stew Beef in Gobbets in the French fashion.

Take a flank of Beef or any part but the leg, cut it into slices or gobbets as big as a pullets egg, with some gobbets of fat, and boil it in a pot or pipkin with som fair spring water, scum it clean, and put to it an hour after it hath boil'd, carrots, parsnips, turnips, great onions, salt, some cloves, mace, and whole pepper, cover it close, and stew it till it be very tender; then half an hour before dinner, put into it some picked time, parsley, winter savory, sweet marjoram, sorrel, and spinage (being a little bruised with the back of a ladle) and some claret wine: then dish it on fine sippets, and serve it to the table hot, garnish it with grapes, barberries, or gooseberries. Sometimes use spices, the bottoms of boild artichocks put into beaten butter, and grated nutmeg, garnished with barberries.

Stewed collops of Beef.
Take of the buttock of beef thin slices, cross the grain of the meat, then hack them and fry them in sweet butter, and being fryed fine and brown, put them in a pipkin with some strong broth, a little claret wine, and some nutmeg, stew it very tender; and half an hour before you dish it put to it some good gravy, elder vinegar, and a clove or two: when you serve it put some juyce of orange, and three or four slices on it, stew down the gravy somewhat thick, and put into it when you dish it some beaten butter.

Olines of Beef stewed and roste.
Take a buttock of beef, and cut some of it into thin slices as broad as your hand, then hack them with the back of a knife, lard them with small lard, and season them with pepper, salr[salt?], and nutmeg; then make a farsing with some sweet herbs, time, onions, the yolks of hard eggs, beef suet or lard all minced, some salt, barberries, grapes, or gooseberries; season it with the former spices lightly, and work it up together, then lay it on the slices, and roul them up round with some caul of veal, beef or mutton, bake them in a dish in the oven, or roste them, then put them in a pipkin with some butter, and saffron, or none, blow off the fat from the gravy and put it to them, with some artichocks, potato, or skirrets blanched, being first

boild, a little claret wine, and serve them on sippets, with some slic't orange, lemon, barberries, grapes or gooseberries.

To boil a capon or chicken with Colyflowers.
Cut of the Buds of your flowers, and boil them in milk with a little mace till they be very tender, then take the yolks of 2 eggs, and strain them with a quarter of a pint of sack then take as much thick butter being drawn with a little vinegar and a slic't lemon, brew them together; then take the flowers out of the milk, put them to the butter and sack, dish up your capon being tender boil'd upon sippets finely carved, and pour on the sauce, serve it to the table with a little salt.

To boil a Capon or Chicken with Sparagus.
Boil your Capon or Chicken in fair water and some salt, then put in their bellies a little mace, chopped parsley, and sweet butter; being boiled, serve them on sippets, and put a little of the broth on them: then have a bundle or two of sparagus boild, put in beaten butter, and serve it on your Capon or chicken.

A rare Fricase.
Take six pidgeon and six chicken peepers, scald and trusse them being drawn clean, head and all on, then set them and have some lamb-stones and sweetbreads blanched, parboil'd and slic'd, frye most of the sweetbreads flowred, have also some asparagus ready, cut off the tops an inch long, the yolks of wo hard eggs, pistaches, the marrow of six Marrow-bones, half the marrow fryed green, and white batter, let it be kept warm till it be almost dinner time, then have a clean frying pan, and frye the fowl with good sweet butter, being finely fryed put out the butter, and put to them some rost Mutton gravy, some large fryed oysters, and some salt; then put in the hard yolks of eggs, and the rest of the sweetbreads that are

not fryed, the pistaches, asparagus, and half the marrow: then stew them well in the frying pan with some grated nutmeg, pepper (a clove or two of garlick if you please) a little white wine, and let them be well stewed. Then have ten yolks of eggs dissolbed in a dish with grape-verjuice or wine vinegar, and a little beaten mace and put it into the frycase, then have a French six penny loaf slic'd into a fair large dish set on coals, with some good mutton gravy, then give the frycase two or three walms on the fire, and pour it on the sops in the dish; garnish it with fryed sweetbread, fryed oysters, fryed marrow, pistaches, slic'd almonds, and the juice of two or three Oranges.

To boil a Capon, Pullet, or Chicken.
Boil them in good mutton broth, with mace, a faggot of sweet herbs, sage, spinage, marigold leaves and flowers, white or green endive, burrage, bugloss, parsley, and sorrel, and serve it on sippets.

To boile Capons or Chickens *with Sage and Parsley*.
First boil them in water and salt, then boil some parsley, sage, two or three eggs hard, chop them; then have a few thin slices of fine manchet, and stew all together, but break not the slices of bread, stew them with some of the broth wherein the Chickens boils, some large mace, butter, alittle white wine or Vinegar, with a few barberries or grapes; dish up the chickens on the sauce, and run them over with sweet butter and lemon cut like dice, the peel cut like small lard, and boil a little peel with the chickens.

To boil a Capon or Chicken *with divers compositions*.
Take off the skin whole, but leave on the legs, wings, and heads, mince the body with some beef suet or lard, put to it some sweet herbs minced, and season it with cloves, mace, pepper, salt, two or three eggs, grapes, goosberries, or barberries, bits of potato or mushrooms: In the winter with sugar, currans, and prunes fill the

skin, prick it up, and stew it between two dishes, with large mace, and strong broth, pieces of artichocks, cardones or asparagus, and marrow: being finely stewed, serve it on carved sippets, and run it over with beaten butter, [lemon] slic'd, and scrape on sugar.

To boil a Capon, Chicken *with* Cardones *Mushrooms,* Artichocks, *or* Oysters.

The foresaid fowls being parboild and cleansed from the grounds, stew them finely; then take your cardones being cleaned and peeled into water, have a skillet of fair Water boiling hot, and put them therein; being tender boild, take them up and fry them in chopt lard or sweet butter, pour away the butter, and put them into a pipkin, with strong broth, pepper, mace, ginger, verjuice, and [juyce] of orange; stew all together with some strained almonds, and some sweet herbs chopped, give them a walm, and serve your capon or chicken on sippets.

Let them be fearsed, and wrap your searst Fowl in cauls of Veal, half rost them, then stew them in a pipkin with the foresaid cardones and broth.

To boil any Land Fowl, as Turky, Bustard, Pheasant, Peacock, Partridge, or the like.

Take a Turkey and flay off the skin, leave the legs and rumps whole, then mince the flesh raw with some Beef suet or lard, season it with some nutmeg, pepper, salt and some minced sweet herbs, then put to it some yolks of raw eggs, mingle all together with 2 bottoms of boil'd Artichokes, rosted chesnuts blanched, some marrow, and some boil'd skirrets or parsnips cut like dice, or some pleasant pears, and yolks of hard eggs in quarters, some gooseberries, grapes or barberries; fill the skin, and prick it up in the back, stew it in a stewing pan or deep dish, and cover it with another; but first put some strong broth to it, some Marrow, artichocks boyled and quartered, large mace, white wine, chesnuts, quarters of pears, salt, grapes, barberries, and some of the meat made up in balls stewed with the Turkey; being finely boil'd or stewed, serve it on fine carved sippets, broth it, and lay on the garnish with slices of lemon and whole lemon-peel, run it over with beaten butter, and garnish the dish with chesnuts, yolks of hard eggs, and large mace.

For the lears of thickening, yolks of hard eggs strained with some of the broth, or strained almond paste with some of the broth, or else strained bread and sorrel.

Otherwayes you may boil the former fowls either boned and trust up with a farsing of some minced veal or mutton, and seasoned as the former in all points, with those materials, or boil it with the bones in being trust up. A Turkey to bake, and break the bones.

Otherwayes bone the fowl, and fill the body with he foresaid farsing or make a pudding of grated bread, minced suet of Beef or Veal, seasoned with cloves, mace, pepper, salt and grapes, fill the body and prick up the back and stew it as aforesaid.

Or make the pudding of grated bread, beef-suet minced, some currans, nutmegs, cloves, sugar, sweet herbs, salt, juice of spinage; if yellow, saffron, some minced meat, cream, eggs and barberries: fill the fowl and stew it in mutton broth, and white Wine, with the gizard, liver, and bones, stew it down well, then have some artichock bottoms boil'd and quartered, some potatoes boil'd and blanched, and some dates quartered, also some marrow boil'd in water and salt; for the garnish some boil'd skirret or pleasant pears. Then make a lear of almond paste strained with mutton broth for the thickening of the former broth.

Otherwayes simple being stuffed with parsley, serve it in with butter, vinegar, and parsley boiled and minced; as also bacon boiled on it or about it, in two pieces, and two saucers of green sauce.

Or otherwayes for variety, boil your fowl in water and salt, then take strong broth and put in a faggot of sweet herbs, mace, marrow, cucumber slic't, and thin slices of interlarded bacon and salt, &c.

To boil **Capon** *or* **Chicken** *with Sugar Pease.*
When the cods be but young, sting them and them and pick off the husks, then take two or three handfuls and put them into a pipkin with half a pound of sweet butter, a quarter of a pint of fair water, gross, pepper, salt, mace, and some sallet oyl: stew them till they be very tender, and strain to them 3 or 4 yolks of eggs, with six spoonfuls of Sack.

To make a Neats-Tongue Pye.
Take a couple of Neats Tongues and almost boyle them, then cut out the meat at the butt end, as far as you can, not breaking it out at the sides, put a little suet to the said meat you cut out, a few sweet herbs and parsly mingled altogether very small, season it with a little pepper, salt, cloves, mace, ginger, and a handful of grated bread, a little sugar, and the yolks of three or four eggs, mould it up into a body, season tour Tongues in the inside and outside with your seasoning aforesaid, and wash them within with the yolk of an egge, and force them where you cut forth the meat, and make a forced meat of the residue; then having the coffin made in the form of a Neats Tongue, lay them in with the puddings little bales to them, put in dates and shred lemmon with butter on the top, and close it up; when it is baked, put in a lear of the Venison Sawce, which is Claret Wine, a handful of grated bread, cinnamon, ginger, sugar, and a little vinegar, boyl them up so thick, as it may onely run like butter, it ought to be sharp and sweet; this sawce serves for any part of Venison wash'd the Shoulders, Sides and Hannches, which if seasoned, must be laid in water, and when roasted must be served up stuck with rosemary.

To roast a Levret or Hare.

Case your Levret, but cut not off their hinder legs nor ears but hack one leg through another, so likewise cut a whole through one ear, and put it through the other; in the mean time make your Sawce with a little Tyme, Sweet-marjorum, and Winter-savoury very small, with the liver of the Hare boyled, and the yolks of three or four hard eggs, with a little Bacon and beef-suet, boyl this well up with water and vinegar, when it is boyled, add a grated Nutmeg, sweet Butter, and a little Sugar, and dish your Hare; the same may you make to Rabbets.

To Stew Ducks the French fashion.

Take the Duck and half roast it, put half a score oynions in the belly whole, some whole pepper, a bundle of tyme, a little salt, when it is half roasted, take it up and slash it into pieces, put it between two dishes, and pierce the gravy, mix some claret wine with that gravy, and a little sliced nutmeg, a couple of anchovies, wash them and slit them, slice the [onyons] [in] the Ducks belly, cover the dishes close, so let them stew while enough; take some butter, beat it thick and shred a lemmon in it and serve it, garnish your dish with the lemmon peel and your oynions.

To make a Pidgeon Pie.

Truss your Pidgeons to bake, and set them, and lard the one half of them with Bacon, mince a few sweet herbs and parsly with a little beef suet, the yolks of hard eggs, and an onyon or two, season it with salt, beaten pepper, cloves, mace, and nutmeg, work it up with a piece of butter, and stuff the bellies of the Pidgeons, season them with some salt, beaten pepper, cloves, mace, and beaten nutmeg, take also as many lambs stones, seasoned as aforesaid, with six collops of Bacon, (the salt drawn out) then make a round coffin and put in your Pidgeons, and if you will put in lambs stones and sweet breads, and some hartichoke bottoms, or other dry meat to soak up the juyce, because the Pye will be very sweet and full of it, then put a little white wine beaten up with the yolk of an egg when it comes out of the oven, and so serve it.

To boyl pidgeons after the Dutch way.
Take your Pidgeons, set and lard them, put them into a pipkin with so much strong broth, (made of knuckles of veal, and mutton, and beaf) and very well cover them, when they are scummed, put to them a faggot of sweet herbs, some large mace, a handful of capers, and raisins of the sun shred very small, six quartered dates, a piece of butter with three yolks of hard eggs minced, with a handful of grapes or barberies, then beat two yolks of your eggs with verjuice and some white bread, a ladle of sweet butter & a grated nutmeg, so serve it with sippits; though the modern way is to boyl it with colops of bacon, and dish it with rice boyled, carrets and turnips minced small and colliflowers.

To make an Egg Pye, or Mince Pye of Eggs.
Take the yolks of two dozen of eggs, shred them, take the same weight of beef suet, about a pound, half a dozen pippins, a pound of currants well washed and dried, half a pound of sugar, a pennyworth of beaten spice, a few carroway seeds, candid orange peel shred, a little verjuice, some rose-water, fill the coffin, and bake it with a gentle heat.

To make a Sallet of a cold Hen or Pullet.
Take a Hen and roast it, let it be cold, carve up the legs, take the flesh and mince it small, shred a lemmon, a little parsley and onyons, an apple, a little pepper and salt with oyle and vinegar, garnish the dish with the bones and lemmon peel, and so serve it.

To make a Hash of Capon or Pullet.

Take a Capon or Partridge and roast them, and being cold, mince them very fine, the brains and wings, and tear the leggs and rumps whole to be carbonadoed, then put some strong mutton broth or good gravy, greated nutmeg, a great onyon and salt, then stew them in a large earthen pipkin or sauce-pan, stew the rumps and legs in the same strong broth in another pipkin, then take some light French bread chipt, and cover the bottom of the dish, steep the bread in the same broth, or good mutton gravy, then pour the hash on the steeped bread, lay the legs and the rump on the hash, with some fryed oysters, sliced lemmon, and lemmon peel, the juyce of orange, and yolks of eggs strained, and beaten butter, garnish the dish with carved oranges, lemmons, &c. thus you may hash any kind of foul; there are other whimsical ingredients in the practise of Cookery, but I mention onely such as have a ready and natural, not forced or forraign relish, which was little used here.

To butter Eggs upon Toasts.

Take twenty Eggs, beat them in a dish with some salt, and put butter to them, then have two large Rolls or fine Manchets, cut them in Toasts and toast them against the fire with a pound of fine sweet butter, being finely butter'd in a fare clean dish; put the eggs on the toasts, and garnish your dish with pepper and salt, otherwayes half boyle them in the shells, then butter them, and serve them on toasts or toasts about them.

To Stew a Line, Leg, Breast of Mutton.

Take a loyn of Mutton and joynt it well, and do so to the breast, and draw and stuff it with sweet herbs and minced parsley, then put it in a deep stewing dish, with the right side downwards, put to it so much white wine and strong broth as will stew it, set it on a great heap of coals, put in two or three onyons, a bundle of sweet herbs, and a little large mace, when it is almost stewed, take a handful of spinnage, parsley and endive and put into it, at the last you may put some gooseberries or grapes; in the winter time sampiere and capers, here you may add them at any time, dish up the loyn of Mutton and put by the liquor you do not [use], and thicken the other with yolks of eggs and sweet butter, so put on the sauce and the herbs over the meat, and garnish the dish with lemmon and barberries.

To hash a Rabbet.
You must take the flesh from the bones of the Rabbet, being before washed, and mince it small with your mincing knife, so put to it a little vinegar, an oynion or two, with a grated nutmeg, and let it stew up together, then mince a handful of boyled parsley green, with a lemmon cut like dice, and a few barberries, putt it into the Harsh, and toste it altogether, and when it is enough, put a ladleful of sweet butter to it, and dish it upon the lines, so garnish it with lemmon.

To Carbonado Mutton.
Boyl a shoulder or breast of Mutton, then scorch them with your knife, and strew on minced tyme and salt, and a little nutmeg, when they are boiled, dish them up; the sauce is claret wine boyled up with two oynions, a little samphiere and capers, and a little gravy, garnish with lemmons.

To pickle Oysters.
Take a quart of the largest great Oysters, with the liquor, wash them clean, and wipe them, add to them a pint of fair water, with half a pint of whit wine vineger, half an ounce of whole pepper, an handful of salt, a quarter of an ounce of large mace, with the liquor of the Oysters strained, put altogether in a pipkin over a soft fire, let them simper together a quarter of an hour; when the Oysters are enough, take them up and put them into a little fair water and vinegar,

until they be cold, the pickle boyling a quarter of an hour after the Oysters are taken up, both being cold put them up together; when you use them, garnish the dish with barberries and lemmon, and a little of the mace and pepper, and pour in some of the pickle.

"These Oysters look like they are off..."

A way to fry Rabbets with sweet sauce.

Cut your Rabbet in pieces, wash it and dry it well in a cloth, take some fresh butter and fry the Rabbet in it, when your Rabbet is little more then half fryed, take some slices of shred very small, a quarter of a pint of cream, the yolks of a couple of egges, some grated nutmeg and salt; when the Rabbet is enough, put them into the pan, and stir them altogether, take a little vinegar, fresh butter and sugar, melt it together, and so serve it with sippets, the dish garnished with flowers, &c.

How to roast a Rabbet with Oysters.

Wash your Rabbet and dry it well, take half a pint of Oysters, wash them and wipe them clean one by one, and put them into the Rabbets belly, a couple of oynions shred, whole pepper, latge macee, two or three sprigs of tyme, sow up the belly: for the sauce as usual, the liver and parsley, a hard egge, shred them together, and beat some butter thick, put it into the dish and serve it.

To make a Frickasse of Chickens.

Take three or four Chickens, scalt them, flea off the skin and feathers together, put them in a little water, take halfe a pint of white wine, and two or three whole oynions, some large mace and nutmeg tyed up in a cloth, a bundle of sweet herbs and a little salt, and put them all in a pipkin closely covered, let them simmer a quarter of an hour, then take half a dozen yolks of eggs, half a pound of sweet butter, four anchovies dissolved in a little of the broth, shred your boyled spice small, take a quarter of a pound of capers, shred them very small, put the anchovies dissolved into the egges and butter and capers, and so stir it altogether over a chafing-dish of coals, till it begin to thicken, then take the Chicken out of the broth and pour lear upon them, serve them with sippets and lemmon sliced.

Another way to fry the same Fricasse brown.

Take four Chickens, scald them and cut them in quarters, beat them flat with your cleaver, and break their bones, dry them with a cloth very well, and flower them all over on the skinny sides, your pan being hot with clarified butter, put them in with the skinny sides downwards, fry them brown, then turn them, let your lear be a little claret wine and gravy, then put your liquor out of your pan, and put it in your lear, with peices of sassages wrung off as long as your thumb, and a pint of oysters, two or three oynions, with a bundle of sweet herbs, a grated nutmeg, and two or three anchovies, let them boyl up in the pan, then beat he yolks of four eggs, with a little strong broth, take the pan off the fire and put them in, if it turns too thick, you may thin it with wine, gravy or strong broth, keep it shaking whilst it's on the fire; then dish up your Chickens in sippets, and pour on your lear and oysters, with your pieces of sassages by the sides of the dish, and garnish it with lemmon.

A grand Sallet.
Take a quarter of a pound of raisons of the sun, a quarter of a pound of blancht almons,, a quarter of a pound of capers, a quarter of a pound of olives, the like quantity of samphiere, aquarter of a pound of pickle cucumbers, a lemmon shred, some pickled French beans, a wax tree set in the middle of the dish, pasted to the dish, lay all their quarters round the dish (you may also mince the flesh of a roasted hen, with sturgeon and shrimps) and garnish the dish with cut beans and turnips in several figures.

How to pickle French-beans.
Take your Beans and string them, boyl them tender, then take them off, and let them stand till they are cold, put them into the pickle of beer-vinegar, pepper and salt, cloves and mace, with a little ginger.

A Cordial strengthening Broth.
Take a red Cock, strip off the feathers with the skin, take a rolling-pin and bruise his bones to shivers, set it over the fire and just cover it with water, put in some salt, and watch the scumming and boyling of it, put in a handful of harts-horn, a quarter of a pound of blew currants, as many stoned raisins of the sun, as many pruens, four blades of large mace, a bottom crust of a white-loaf, half an ounce of china-root sliced, being steeped three hours before in warm water, boyl in three or four pieces of gold, strain it and put in a little fine sugar and juice of orange and so use it.

Another way.

Take a Cock or two, cut off their wings and legs, cleanse all the blood out of the inside, par-boyl them very well, that when they are boyled, there may arise no scum, then wash them again in fair water, put them in a pitcher with a pint of Rhenish wine, and as much of your aforesaid strong broth as will cover them, add thereto a few cloves, large mace, shred ginger and nutmeg, a little whole pepper, with a small quantity of china, and an ounce or two of harts-horn, put a little salt and stop up your pitcher close that no steam may come forth; you must boyl the pitcher in a great pot about six hours, then pour out the broth and strain it into a bason, and scruze into it the juice of two or three lemmons. These were [her] ordinary morning draughts, with caudles, for variety, of the Proctectress and her Master, and about 11 a clock, a cup full of small Ale with a toast and sugar.

How to make Barley-broth.

Take Barley and put in fair water, give it three qualms over the fire, separate the waters, and put it into a cullender, boyl it in a fourth water, with a blade of mace and a clove, and when it is boyled away, put in some raisins and currants, and when the fruit is boyled enough, take it off and season it with white wine, rose-water, butter and sugar, and a couple of yolks of egges beaten with it: This was a Mess frequently prepared for *Oliver*.

To make a Pudding of Hogs Liver another way.

Boyl your Hogs Liver and grate it, put to it more grated bread then Liver, with as much fine flower, as of either, put twelve eggs to the value of a gallon of this mixture, with about two pound of beef suet minced small, with a pound and a half of currants, half a quarter of a pint of rose-water, a good quantity of cloves and mace, nutmeg, cinnamon, and ginger, all minced very small, mix all these with sweet milk and cream, let it be no thicker then fritter batter; To fill your Hogs guts, you may make with it the maw fit to be eaten hot at Table; in your kniting or tying the guts, you must remember to give them three or four inches scope: In your putting them into the boyling water, you must handle them round, to bring the meat equal to all parts of the gut, they will ask about half an hour boyling, the boyling must be sober, if the wind rise in them, you must be ready to prick them, or else they will flie and burst in pieces; This was Madam *Frances* her Delicacy.

How to make an Eele Pie, with Oysters.

Take the Eels, wash them and gut them, and dry them well in a cloath, to four good Eles allow a pint of Oysters well washed, season them with pepper, salt, and nutmeg, and large mace, put half a pound of butter into the Pie, as also half a lemmon sliced, so bake it, when it is drawn, take the yolks of two Eggs, a couple of anchovies dissolved in a in a little white wine, with a quarter of a pound of fresh butter, met it, and mix altogether and make a Lear out of it, and put it into the Pie.

How to roast a Shoulder of Mutton with Oysters.

Your Oysters being parboild, put to them some parsley, tyme, and winter savoury minced small, with the yolks of six eggs hard boiled and minced, a half-penny-loaf of grated bread, three or four yolks of eggs, so mingle all together with your hands, your Shoulder of Mutton being spitted, lay it upon the dresser and make holes with a sticking knife, in it (you may cut the holes as wide as you think convenient) put in your Oysters with the herbs and ingredients after them, about thirty Oysters will be enough; let it roast indifferent long, take the rest of a quart and put them into the deep dish, with claret wine, two or three onyons, in halves, a couple of minced anchovies, put all this under your Mutton in the pan, so save your gravie, and when your meat is ready, put your sauce upon a heap of coals, put to it the yolk of an egg beaten, a grated nutmeg and sweet butter, dish the Shoulder of Mutton, and pour this thick lear of Oysters all over it, and garnish it with barbaries and lemmons.

How to pickle up Cucumbers.

Take young Gerkins, and wipe them clean, take the seeds of dill and fennel, large mace, beaten pepper and salt, season the beer vineger very well with salt, lay a layer of cucumbers, and sprinkle between every row of Cucumbers, your seeds and seasoning; When the pot is almost full with Cucumbers, fill it up to the brim with beer vineger, and keep it close covered; If you like broom buds rather, they are to be pickled only with water and salt, and shut close as before; But I may add (to put the Cariors nose out of joynt that onyons and water were the chief Court sauce, and shall hence forth be exalted and dignified by the name of the Protectors Hogo.

How to make a fresh Cheese.

I have mentioned before her making of Butter, I shall now give you an Experiment of her making of fresh Cheese. Take some new milk or cream, and a race of cinnamon, scald it, then take it off the fire, sweeten it with fine suger, then take a spoonful of runnet to two quarts of milk, set it by and keep it close covered, and so let it stand, when the cheese comes, strow a little fine sugar, and grated nutmeg, and serve it in with sippits, sops in Sack or Muscadine; which at this season of the year, was one of the extempore entertainments of this rustical Lady.

To roast a Lamb, or Kid.

Truss your Lamb or Kid, pricking the head backwards over the shoulder, laying it down, set it and lard it with Bacon, and draw it with time, and a little lemmon peel, then make a pudding with a little grated bread, a handful of sweet herbs, a handful of beef suet, put in about a handful of flower, and a little sassage with time, made mince meat, , season it with cloves, mace, cinamon, ginger, nutmeg, and salt, make it up into a tender body, with two or three eggs, and a little bran, stuff it into the belly of the Lamb, and Kid, put some sauce of Veal or Lamb over it, so prick it up the belly, [roast] the Lamb and Kid, and when it is enough, serve it up with Venison sauce.

To roast Venison.
This is the same common way with roasting a Hogs harslet, and meerly devised, for to take off by its variety the nauseousness of this meat, which was in abundance at their Table, as shall further be manifested. Take the biggest part of the Hanch of venison, and cut it in thin collops, hack it with your knife, as you do the like to Veal, then lard it very thick, with a small larding pin, then take a handful of parsley and spinnage, good store of tyme, a little Rosemary, winter-savoury and sweet marjorum, mince it exceeding small, with a little beef-suet, so put it in the dish with your Venison; put to it some beaten cloves, cinnamon, nutmeg, with a pretty quantity of salt, the yolks of half a dozen egges or more, mingle it up altogether with your hands, then spit your colops on a small spit or long *broaches* made with sticks, you must spit them so by doubling of them or bringing in the ends, that they may not hang too long, but equal; when they are all spitted, put your herbs amongst them and tye them together with a pack-thread; as they roast put a dish under them with claret wine; when they are almost done, take your dish and set it on the coals, put grated bread, beaten cinnamon, vinegar and sugar to the wine, with a ladleful of drawn butter, dish up your Venison, and put on this lear, but very thin over it, and so serve it.

How to boyl a Hanch of Venison.

This was a truly Royal and constant dish in its season at Court, when it was so really, and therefore out of curiosity and state was served up to her Table during the season; it is more extraordinary then any of the former, but since her times destroyed the game, yet cheapened and aviled the Venison, and made it every ones meat; which sordid example yet prevails among some proprietors of parks: I will set down this Direction.

First, stuff your Venison with a handful of sweet herbs and parsley minced, with a little beef-suet, and yolks of egges boyled hard, season your stuffing with pepper, nutmeg, ginger and salt, put your Hanch of Venison a boyling, being powdered before, then boyl up three or four colly-flowers in strong broth, & a little milk; when they are boyled, put them forth into a pipkin, add to them drawn butter, and keep them warm by the fire, them boyl up two or three handfuls of spinnage in the same liquor, when it is boyled up, pour out part of your broth, and put in a little vinegar, a ladleful of sweet butter, and a grated nutmeg, your dish being ready with sippets in the bottom, put on the spinnage round towards your dish side, then take up the Venison being boyled, and put it in the middle of your dish, and put in your colly-flowers, and garnish it with barberries, and the brims of the dish with some green parsley minced; cabbage is as good done in the same manner as colly-flowers.

How to bake a Venison-Pasty.

This is called the King of dainties, which *Oliver* stole by retail, (as he did a more real Regality) may years before, and shared this sovereign delicacy among his Complices, but now more then bold *Robin Hood*, he was Lord and avowed Master of the Game, and therefore that his fellow Dear stealers may know how to dress their prey *a la mode Cromwellian*, take this Prescription, for to other persons it will be of no use: when you have powdered your Hanch of Venison, or the sides of it, by taking away all the bones and sinews, and the skin or fat, season it with pepper and salt only, beat it with your rolling-pin, and proportion it for the Pasty, by taking away from one part and adding to another; you're your paste being made with a peck of fine flower, and about three pound of butter, and a dozen eggs, work it up with cold water into as stiff a paste as you can, drive it forth for your Pasty, let it be as thick as a man's thumb, roll It[*sic*] up upon a rolling-pin, and put under it a couple of sheets of cap-paper well flowered, then your white being already minced and beaten with water, proportion it upon the Pasty, to the bredth and length of the Venison, so lay you Venison in the said white, wash it round with your feather, and put on a border; season your Venison at the top, and turn over your other leaf of paste, so close it up together by the rolling-pin, by rolling it up and down by the sides and ends; and when you have flourisht your garnishing, and edged your pasty, vent it at the top, set it into the Oven, and after four or five hours baking, at least, draw it. This will serve, abating the time, for any other

17th century woodcut of a family dining.

meats baking, for beef or mutton, and may be applied, which is the main design of this discovery, to vulgar use. I must omit Her manner of collecting Venison, because not practicable among mean people.

To boyl any usual joint of Meat.

Cut any of them in such large pieces as you usually do a neck of mutton, as that two or three of them may serve in a dish, and put them into a pot, with so much water as will cover them; if you have a line of mutton (the suet taken from it), or a neck of veal, you may take ten sprigs of winter-savoury, and as much of tyme, adding to them twelve great onyons, if they are small, take the more, grate to them half a penny loaf, with half an ounce of cloves and mace, and one handful of spinnage, a little salt and parsley (if in the Spring or Summer, otherwise capers and samphiere) let it boyl moderately, until it be half consumed; when you take it off, add a little vinegar and sweet butter, but you must not let your spinnage and parsley have above a quarter of an hours boyling.

To bake Steaks the French way.

Season the Steaks with pepper, nutmeg and salt lightly, and set them by, then take a piece of the leanest of a leg of mutton and mince it small with some beef-suet, and a few sweet herbs, as tops of tyme and penny-royal, grated bread, yolks of eggs, sweet cream, raisins of the sun, &c. work all these together, and make it into little balls or puddings, put them (into a deep round pye) on th Steaks, then put to them some butter, and sprinkle it with verjuice, close it up and bake it, when it is enough, cut it up and liquor it with the juice of two or three oranges or lemmons.

To bake a Pig.

This is an experiment practised by Her at *Huntingdon* Brewhouse, and is a singular and the only way of dressing a Pig. Take a good quantity of clay, such as they stop barrels bungs with, and having moulded it, stick your Pig; and blood him well, and when he is warm, arm him like a Curassier, or one of *Cromwels* Iron-sides, hair, skin and all (his intrails drawn and belly sowed up again) with this prepared clay, thick every where, then throw him below the stoak-hole under the Furnace, and there let him soak, turn him now and then, then the clay is hardened, for twelve hours, he is then sufficiently baked; then take him and break off the clay, which easily parts, and you will have a fine crispy coat, and all the juice of the Pig in your dish; remember but to put a few leaves of sage, and a little salt in the belly of it, and you need no other sauce. The like you may do with any fowle whatsoever, for the clay will fetch off and consume the feathers.

Another way according to Court fashion.

Flay a small fat Pig, cut it in quarters, or in smaller pieces, season it with pepper, ginger and salt, lay it into a fit coffin, strip and mince small a handful of parsley, six sprigs of winter-savoury, strew it on the meat in the Pye, and strew upon that the yolks of three or four hard eggs minced, and lay upon them five or six blades of mace, a handful of clusters of barberries, a handful of currants well washed and picked, a little sugar, half a pound of sweet butter or more, close your Pye and set it in an Oven, as hot as for manchet, and in three hours it will be baked, draw it forth, and put in half a pint of sugar, being warmed upon the fire, pour it all over the meat, and put on the pye lid again, scrape on sugar, and serve it hot on the Table.

To make a Fool.

Take two quarts of cream, set it over the fire and let it boyl, then take the yolks of twelve eggs and beat them very well with three or four spoonfuls of cold cream, and then strain the eggs in the skillet of the hot cream, stirring it all the time to keep it from burning, then set it on the fire, and let it boyl a little while, but keep it still stirring for fear of burning, so then take it off, and let it stand and cool, then take two or three spoonfuls of sack, and put it in the dish, with four or five sippets, set the dish and sippets a drying, and when they be dry that they hang to the dish, sweeten the cream and pour it into the dish softly, because the sippets shall not rise up; this will make three dishes, when it is cold it is fit to be eaten.

To make an Artichoak-Pye.
Take the bottom of six Artichoaks, being boyled very tender, put them in a dish, and some vinegar over them, season them with ginger and sugar, a little mace whole, and put them in a coffin of paste: when you lay them in, lay some marrow and dates sliced, & a few raisins of the sun in the bottom, with good store of butter, when it is half baked, take a gill of sack, being boyled first with sugar, and a pill of orange, put it in the Pye, and set it in the Oven again till you use it.

To boyl Flounders or Jacks after the best manner.
Take a pint of white wine, the tops of young tyme and rosemary, and a little whole mace, a little whole pepper seasoned with verjuice, salt, and a piece of sweet butter, and so serve it; you may do fish in the same liquor three or four times.

To draw Butter, of only use in sauces.
Take the butter and cut it into thin slices, put it into a dish, then put it upon the coals where it may melt leisurely, stir it often, and when it is melted, put in two or three spoonfuls of water or vinegar whichever you please, then stir it and beat it until it be thick, if the colour keep white it is good, but if it look yellow and curdly in boyling, it is nought, and not fit to be used to this purpose.

To make puff-paste.

Break two egges in three pits of flower, make it with cold water, then rowl it out pretty thick and square, then take so much butter as paste, and divide your butter in five places, that you may lay it on at five several times, rowl your paste very broad, and take one part of the same butter in little pieces all over your paste, then throw a handful of flower slightly on, then fold up your paste, and beat it with a rolling-pin, so rowl it out again; thus do several times and then make it up.

To make an excellent Jelly.

Take three gallons of fair water, boyl in it a knuckle of veal, and two calves feet slit in two, with all the fat clean taken from between the clawes, so let them boyl to a very tender Jelly keeping it clean scummed, and the edges of the pot always wiped with a clean cloth, that none of the scum may boyl in them, strain it from the meat, and let it stand all night, and the next morning take away the top and the bottom, and take to a quart of this Jelly half a pint of sherry sack, half an ounce of cinnamon, and as much sugar as will season it, six whites of eggs very well beaten; mingle all these together, then boyl it half an hour, and let it run through your Jelly bag.

Another manner to make a fresh Cheese presently.

Take the whites of six eggs, beat them very well, and ring in the juice of a good lemmon to the whites, when the cream seetheth up, put in the whites and stir it about till it be turned, and then take it off and put it into a cheese trough, and let the whay be drawn from it, then take the curd and pound it in a stone morter, with a little rose-water and sugar, and put it into an earthen cullender, and so let it stand till you send it to the Table, then put it into a dish, and put a little cream to it, and so serve it.

Mrs Cromwell's Cookbook

To make a Cheese-cake the best way.

Take two gallons of new milk, put into it two spoonfuls and a half of runner, heat the milk little less then blood-warm, cover it close with a cloth, until you see the cheese be gathered, then with a scumming dish gently take out the whay, so when you have drained the curd as clean as you can, put the curd into a sieve, and let it drain very well there, then to two quarts of curd take a quart of thick cream, a pound of sweet butter, twelve eggs, a pound and a half of currants, a penny worth of clove, nutmeg and mace beaten, half a pound of good sugar, a quarter of a pint of rose-water, so mingle it well together, and put it in puff-paste.

Another way.

Put due quantity of runnet to three gallons of milk, that it it[*sic*] may be a tender curd, run it through a thin strainer, when it comes or gathereth, squeese or pres out the whay, as well as you can possible, put it into a deep bason, put to it about a pound of sweet

Much cooking still to be done...

butter melted, sixteen eggs, casting away half the whites, season it with beaten cinnamon, ginger, cloves, mace and nutmeg, some sugar sufficient to sweeten it, with some salt, eringo and citron minced, a handful of grated bread or naples biskit, mix it all well together, if it be too stiff add a little sweet cream, let it not be too thin, so beat down the sides of your cakes; then make your cakes with melted butter, and warm your milk, with a handful of poudered sugar, rowl out your paste, and jag out your pattern by a large round trencher and paper thereon, then put on the seasoned curds by spoonfuls, and turn up the sides of it in six or eight corners, bake them in a quick Oven, but not too hot. They will ask a quarter of an hours baking.

To broyl Oysters.
Take the biggest Oysters you can get, then take a little minced tyme, grated nutmeg, and grated bread, and a little salt, put this to the Oysters, then get some of the largest bottom shells and place them on the gridiron, and put two or three oysters in each shell, then put some butter to them, and let them simmer on the fire till the liquor bubbles low, supplying it still with butter, when they are crisp, feed them with white wine, and a little of their own liquor, with a little grated bread, nutmeg and minced tyme, but as much only to relish it, so let it boyl up again, then add some drawn butter to thicken them, and dish them on a dish or plate, but if you have scollop shells it is the best way to broyl them in.

To broyl Scollops.
First boyl the Scollops, and then take them out of the shells and wash them, then slice them and season hem with nutmeg, ginger and cinnamon, and put them into the bottom of your shells again, with a little butter, white wine and vinegar, and grated bread, let them be boyled on both sides; if they are sharp, they must have sugar added to them, for the fish is luscious and sweet naturally; there is

therefore another proper way to broyl them, with Oyster liquor and gravy, with dissolved anchovies, minced onyons and tyme, with the juice of a lemmon in it.

To stew a dish of Trouts.

Let your frying-pan be very hot with clarified butter, then split them in two, and give them a sudden brown with a forcible heat, and let a stewing dish be ready prepared with gravy, oyster liquor, a little claret wine and vinegar, fry three or four sliced onyons, and when they are brown, put them to the fish, with a handful of parsley fryed green, a sliced nutmeg, two or three anchovies, and let it just boyl up together, then dish up your Trouts upon sippets; notwithstanding the best way for crispness and and fight of your fish, is to fry the split fish as Trout, Salmon Peel, and Salmon very crisp and brown; dish it up with the inside uppermost

To stew a Carp.

Take a living Carp and knock him on the head, open him in the belly and take heed you break not the gall, pour in a little vinegar, and wash out all the blood, stir it about with your hand, then keep it safe, then have a pan or skillet on the fire, with so much white wine as will almost cover the fish; put to it an onyon cut in the middle, a clove or less of garlick, a race of ginger shred, a nutmeg quartered, a faggot or bundle of sweet herbs, three or four anchovies, your Carp being cut out and rubbed all over with salt, when the wine (if abated with a little water will do as well) doth boyl, put the Carp in, and cover him close, and let him stew up for about a quarter of an hour, then put in the blood and vinegar with a little butter, so dish up the Carp, and let the spawn, milt and revet be laid upon it, the liquor that boyled him, with the butter, is the best sauce, and is to be eaten as broth; garnish the dish with lemmons and grated bread.

To make a Warden or Pear Pye.

Bake your Wardens or pears in an Oven, with a little water and a good quantity of sugar, let your pot be covered with a piece of dough, let then not be fully baked by a quarter of an hour, when they are cold make a high coffin, and put them in whole, adding to them some cloves, whole cinnamon, sugar with some of the liquor they were closed in, so bake it.

To make a Quince Pye.

Cut your Quinces from the core, and fill your pye, lay over it sliced oringado, and pour into it the syrrup of barberries, mulberries, oringado, and put on good store of sugar, with two or three sticks of cinnamon, so close and prick it, but give it as little vent as you can; you may also bake them whole, after you have cored them with your coring iron and pared them very thin, when they are placed in your Pye, fill the vacant place where your core was taken out, with the syrrup of orangado, they ought to have as much sugar as their weight, but not if you have store of sweet syrrup.

To make a Pye with Pippins.

You must core and pare your pippins, and when your coffin is made, take a handful of sliced quinces and strew over the bottom thereof, then place in your pippins, and fill the core holes with the syrrup of quinces, and put into every one a piece of oringado, so pour on the syrrup of quinces over the apples with sugar, and close it; these Pyes will ask good soaking, especially the quince Pye.

To make a double Tart.

Take some codlings tenderly boyled and peel them, cut them I halves, fill your Tart, put into a quarter of a hundred of codlings a pound and a half sugar, a few cloves, and a little cinnamon, close up the coffin and bake it; when it comes out of the oven, take a quart of cream, six eggs, a quartern of sugar and a sliced nutmeg, beat all these well together, pour them into the Tart, then set your Tart in the Oven for half a quarter of an hour, when it comes out, cut off the ley and having a lid cut in flowers ready, lay it on , and garnish it with preserves of damsons, resberries, apricocks and cherries, and place a preserved quince in the middle, and strew it with sugar biskets.

How to make an Almond Tart.
Raise an excellent good past with six corners, an inch deep, take some blancht Almonds very finely beaten with rose-water, take a pound of sugar to a pound of Almonds, some grated nutmeg, a little cream, with strained spinnage as much as will colour the Almonds green, so bake it with a gentle heat in an Oven not shutting the lid, draw it, and stick it with candid Orange and Citron, and red and white muscadine.

To make white Quince Cakes.
First clarify the sugar with the white of an egg, but put not so much water to it as you do for Marmalade; before you clarify it, keep out almost a quarter of the sugar, let your Quinces be scalded, and let them be chopped in small pieces before you put it in to the syrrup, then make it boyl as fast as you can, and when you have scummed it, and you think it be half boyled, then jamire it, and let the other part of your sugar be ready candy'd to a hard candy, and so put them together, letting it boyl but a very little after the candy is put to it, then put in a little Musk, and so lay it out before it be cold.

To make red Quince Cakes.
Bake them in an Oven with some of their own juice, their own coars being cut or bruised and put to them, then weigh some of this juice with some of the Quince, being cut into small pieces taking their weight in sugar, and with the Quince, some pritty quantity of

juice of Barberies, being baked or stewed in a pot; when you have taken their weight in sugar, you must put the weighed Quince, and above three quarters of the sugar together, and put to it some little quantity of water as you shall see cause, but make not the syrrup too thinne; and when you have put all this together, cover it, and set it to the fire, keep it covered, and skimme it as much as you can; when it is half boyled, then simmer it; let the other part of sugar have no more water put to it, then well wet the sugar, and so let it be boyled to a very hard candy, and when you think they be boyled enough, then lay them out before they be cold.

To make clear Cakes of Quince.

You must prepare the Quinces and Barberies as before , and then take the clearest syrrup, and let it stand on the coals two or three hours, the take the weight of it in sugar, and put near half the sugar to the juice, and so let them boyl a little on the fire, and then candy the rest of the sugar very hard, and so put them together, stirring it while it is almost cold, and so put it into glasses.

To Preserve Quinces white.

Take to every pound of Quince, a pound an[*sic*] a quarter of sugar, clarify this sugar with the white of an egge, coar your Quinces but not too much, and then put this sugar, and water, and Quince, being raw, together, and so make them boyl so fast as you can see no Quince, but forget not to turn them, and take off what skimme you can, keep them boyling thus fast, till you think they be ENOUGH.

AND so I have run through the whole and more usual fare of her private Table, observing no method therein, because I had them in this form from a near servant of hers? As for Fish and Flesh days, there was no observation of them, all days being alike to the Caterer and Purveyour, and those that eat at her Tables, as was hinted before.

Bu this habit of Diet, not proving effectual to the prolongation of *Olivers* life, by and with which this Court subsisted, and was the onely ligament of that riffraff Society; a Voyder was the next service; for though there were some faint and slight shewes of Housekeeping, which the standing Court Officers maintained with their credit (and injury of several persons, who trusted upon the greatness of the deceased Usurper) to keep their places warm, and themselves in action; yet Mrs. *Cromwel*, wifely and timely withdrew her stake, and suffered her Son *Ricardo*, to run the resque of the old and new debt upon his own Score.

And upon his account, merely was that costly solemnity of *Olivers* Funerals advised, on purpose to bankrupt him: the pomp bestowed on the dead, proving the ruine and disgrace of the living; so that all things went backward with him with double the pace they flowed upon his Father, and I the same manner; for whereas his Father was wont to call in the Guards, to eat the reliques of his Victuals, now they rushed in, and perforce took the meat off his Table, with a demand of their Pay and Arrears, and this with so much insolence, that Mrs. *Cromwel*, the afflicted mother of this Unfortunatus, could not forbear in anger to tell her son *Fleetwood*, That *he had brought his hoggs to a fair Market*: nor is all that Droll, which is mentioned of her in a Play, called *The Rump, or Mirror of the Times.*

FINIS.

Portrait of Oliver Cromwell by Sir Peter Lely; a copy of the famed 'warts and all' portrait.

Glossary of terms and significant figures mentioned in the text

Ambergris — a grey substance like dried putty produced from the secretion of the sperm whale. It has a perfume like the blending of new mown hay with the scent of violets.

Aviled — degraded

Barberries — oblong, red, sharply acid berries, the fruit of the shrub 'Berberis vulgaris'. As well as being used in the kitchen barberries were also used medicinally for ailments of the gall bladder, liver, and kidneys it is interesting to note that Oliver Cromwell suffered with kidney stones.

Barkstead, Sir John — (d.1662) was a London goldsmith who became an officer in the Parliamentarian army and served was one of King Charles I's judges in 1649. He was knighted in 1656 and appointed steward of Cromwell's household. In 1660 he fled to Holland but was arrested in Holland, returned to England and executed.

Basing House — was a grand mansion located in the village of Basing in Hampshire, built by the 1st Marquis of Winchester. It was famous for its stout resistance under the 5th Marquis to the Parliamentarian forces in three sieges over two years. The defenders finally yielded to Cromwell himself in 1645, when architect indigo Jones was one of the prisoners taken. Little now remains of what may have been the grandest house in England, except the 16th century gatehouse and dovecote, and huge Civil War earthworks.

Beaten Ginger	root ginger, well bruised. Many recipes contain 'beaten' spices; the spice was no doubt pounded with a pestle and mortar.
Beer-vinegar	malt vinegar
Blue currents	dry currants, which are small dried black grapes
Borage	'Borago officinalis', mostly used today in summer wine cups and drinks. Has a strong onion-like smell and a spicy cucumber-like taste. Medicinally it is good for the kidneys as it has a mildly diuretic effect.
Bowcher, Elizabeth	Mrs Cromwell's maiden name, usually spelt Bourchier.
Brewis	bread soaked in gravy.
Broach	a tapering pointed instrument, a spit for roasted meat.
Broom buds	'Sarothamnus scoparius' – the common yellow broom of the hedgerows in lime-free soil. Now regarded as unreliable and only to be used under medicinal supervision.
Bugloss	'Echium vulgare' – coarse hairy leaves and blue flowers. The young shoots may be treated and eaten like spinach.
Bustard	the Great Bustard sometimes called the 'Fen Bustard'. A large bird which resembled a Turkey, once common in East Anglia but now extinct.
Capers	the pickled flower buds of a bramble-type Mediterranean shrub. In this country pickled nasturtium seeds are also used as a substitute.
Cap-paper	a kind of course paper, wrapping paper.
Carbonadoed	meat scored with a knife before cooking.
Cardoon or Cardone	'Cynara cardunculus' – a plant closely related to the artichoke, grown for its celery like stalks. Culti-

vated in Europe and introducing to England about 1656.

Case   to skin.

Caudle   a warm drink consisting of thin gruel mixed with wine or ale, sweetened and spiced.

Caul   the net-like fatty membrane which encloses the intestines of the animal. Sometimes used today to wrap meat for barbecue cooking.

Chafing-dish   a vessel to hold burning charcoal, for warming food at the table.

China or China-root   a plant (Smilax China) closely akin to the Sarsaparilla, the powdered root of which is still used as a tonic and blood purifier.

Citron   a Mediterranean fruit 'Citrus medica' somewhat resembling a lemon. The name is now restricted to a pale-yellow oval fruit, larger and less acid than a lemon; but in the 17th century 'citron' would have included both lemon and lime.

Claypole, Elizabeth   was Oliver Cromwell's second daughter and favourite child, known to the family as 'Betty'. She was born in Huntingdon in 1629 and married John Claypole of Northborough Manor at Ely in 1646. Elizabeth died, probably of cancer, at the age of 29; her grief-stricken father survived her by barely a month. She was buried in Westminster Abbey and her tomb allowed to remain there after the Restoration.

Claypole, John   (1625 – 1688) was a country gentleman, the owner of Northborough Manor near Peterborough. Although not in military man he supported the Parliamentarian cause, fighting in the Civil War. He was appointed Cromwell's master of horse in 1653. He had married Cromwell's second daughter Elizabeth at Ely in January 1646; after her death and Claypole gave his mother in law Elizabeth, the subject of this book, a home with him at Northborough until her own death in 1665. Claypole died in poverty in London in 1688, having already sold his Northborough estate to Lord Fitzwilliam.

Cock   woodcock.

Codlings   a variety of apple.

Cods   pods.

Coffin   a pie crust, the mould of paste for a pie. This word has been known in this sense since 1420.

Colewort   any plant of the cabbage family.

Collop   a small piece or slice of boneless meat.

Crequi, Duke de   (1623-1687) Charles III of the 'House of Crequi', a French Noble family. He became Duke de Crequi in 1653, fought at the battles of Rocroi and Nordlingen, and became French ambassador at Rome in 1662. It is recorded that while there he quarrelled with the Papal Guard. Later he became Governor of Paris in 1676 and Ambassador to England in 1677.

Cromwell, Frances   Oliver's youngest daughter born at Ely in 1638. She married first Robert Rich, grandson of Lord Warwick, but was widowed after only three months. Later she married again, this time to Sir John Russell of Chippenham. They have many descendants. Francis lived until 1721 and is buried in Saint Nicholas's Church, Chiswick with her sister Mary.

Cromwell, Henry   fourth and youngest son of Oliver Cromwell, born at Huntingdon in 1628. He entered the Parliamentary army and was a Colonel by 1650. He took part in the Irish campaign and became Major General of the forces in Ireland, a member of the Irish council in 1654 and Lord deputy of Ireland in 1657. Henry urged his father to refuse the title of King. He was Governor General of Ireland in 1658, then returned to England on orders of new

	government in 1659 and retired to Cambridgeshire. He died aged 47 on the 23rd of March 1673 and is buried in Wickham Church.
Cromwell, Richard	third son of Oliver Cromwell, born in Huntingdon in 1626. He succeeded his father as Lord Protector in 1658, but then forced to abdicate 9 months later after a military coup. Heavily in debt, he fled to Europe in 1660 to avoid his creditors. He returned to England in the 168s and lived quietly in retirement at Cheshunt until his death in 1712.
Desborough, John	(1608 – 1680) was the second son of James Desborough of Eltisley in Cambridgeshire. He married in 1636 Oliver Cromwell's sister Jane. He served in Cromwell's regiment during the Civil War and rose to become Major General in the Parliamentarian army. He served as one of the Major Generals governing an area of England, opposed Cromwell accepting the crown, and forced Richard Cromwell to resign. He was a member of the disastrous and short-lived military government which followed. Although briefly imprisoned after the Restoration he then lived quietly until his death.
Drawn	difficult to determine whether this means 'infused' or 'drawn from the oven' in several cases.
Drive forth/Drive out	roll out (pastry).
Earthen colander	earthenware (course country pottery) rather than using a metal one.
Elder vinegar	vinegar in which dried elderflowers have been steeped. According to Gerard's *'Herball'* (1597) "being used with meat it stirreth up an appetite".
Eringo	also spelt eryngo: the candid root of sea-holly, 'Eryngium'. A member of the carrot family with a similar taste.
Farcing	forcemeat stuffing.

Mrs Cromwell's Cookbook

Fairfax, Sir Thomas (1612-1671) 3rd Baron Fairfax of Cameron, was a professional soldier who became a general in the Parliamentarian army in 1642 and distinguished himself throughout the Civil War. He reorganised Parliament's forces into what became known as the New Modelled Army, but refused to be a judge at the trial of the execution of Charles I. He headed the Commission sent to Charles II at The Hague 1660 and retired to Yorkshire. He died in 1671 and is buried in Bilborough Church, near York.

Fearce untraceable except as an old spelling of fierce. The sense seems to indicate that the birds should be seared (by a fierce heat?) to remove the feathers.

Figures beans and turnips cut into various decorative shapes.

Flayed skinned – often spelt as 'flead'.

Fleck of pork also spelt 'flick', the inside fat of the pig, which is melted down for lard, or the fat of pork next to the skin.

Fleetwood, Charles (1618 – 1692) Major General in Cromwell's army and his intimate friend. He was the third son of Sir Miles Fleetwood of Aldwinkle in Northamptonshire. In 1652 he married Cromwell's daughter Bridget, the widow of Henry Ireton.

Fried green (marrow) an untraceable phrase. Could mean 'fresh' marrow (from marrow bones). Bones are said to be 'green' if healthy and full of marrow.

Goffe, William (c.1605-c.1679) was a Parliamentarian officer, one of the Kings judges in 1649, Major General for Berkshire, Sussex and Hampshire in 1655 and a member of Cromwell's House of Lords. At the Restoration he fled with his father in law Edward Whalley to Massachusetts, whilst his family remained in England. He and Whalley lived in isolation for three years, before allegedly emerging

	to repel an attack of Native Americans on Hadley in Massachusetts in 1675. He died about 1679.
Grain	the smallest English measure, about 1/7000 part of a pound weight. originally the lights of one grain of wheat.
Gridiron	a frame of iron bars for broiling over a fire.
Groat	a silver coin worth 4 pennies, which was about the size of a modern penny.
Gross	course.
Hackney turnips	Hackney was a market gardening area on the edge of London in the 1600s.
Harts-horn	the buckthorn (Rhamnus catharticus), the berries of which are a powerful laxative.
Hewson, John	(d. 1662) was a soldier and officer in the Parliamentarian army. Before the Civil War he had been a shoemaker, from which he knew the radical John Lilburne. After the Civil War he became an MP, a member of Cromwell's House of Lords and served as one of the King's judges, signing the death warrant in 1649. He fled the country at the Restoration and died in Amsterdam in 1662.
Holyday, Barten	(1593 – 1661) was a clergyman, author and translator of classical poetry.
Interlarded	strips of fat bacon, etc. inserted into lean meat before cooking.
Jacks	small or young pike, sometimes used as a general name for a pike.
Jones, Philip	(1618-1674) was the Welsh parliamentarian governor of Swansea and one of Cromwell's peers. He was controller of the household to Oliver and Richard Cromwell. Jones acquired a large fortune and was charged with corruption by the military party and extreme Republicans; he later made his peace with

the King and was High Sheriff of Glamorgan in 1671.

Jug Out to cut out a rough paper shape for pastry etc. by cutting it round a plate.

Jamire untraceable word but the sense implies 'test for setting'.

Lambstones the testicles of a lamb.

Loading pin a pointed instrument with which meat is pierced and pieces of fat bacon inserted for cooking.

Lear a thickened sauce.

Ley untraceable in this context. The sense seems to indicate "take off the lid that was baked on the pie". Elizabeth Eaton in 'The Cookery of England' writes "in earlier times a pie was often partly cooked with a false lid made of flour and water-crust, which was broken away and replaced by the rich pastry lid, just as we replaced foil with pastry today".

Lines phrase untraceable but not crucial to the recipe.

Manchet the finest kind of wheaten bread.

Mancini, Michele an Italian nobleman who was introduced to the French court following his marriage in 1656 to Girolama Mazarini, the sister of Cardinal Mazarin, the great French statesman. They had many descendants, most of which were involved in French politics.

Marston Moor the largest and bloodiest battle of the Civil Wars fought near York on 2 July 1644, between the royalist army under Prince Rupert and a combined army of Parliamentarians and Scots Covenanters. The latter were victorious but there were heavy losses on both sides.

Maw the stomach of an animal.

Muscadine	a variety of grape or a variety of pear with the flavour or smell of Musk. Wine made from the same.
Muscadoes	probably a misspelling of muscadine (see above).
Musk	glands from musk deer used mainly in perfume and occasionally in confectionery.
Naples biscuit	not known exactly, obviously a cake or biscuit peculiar to Naples or Italy. The *Oxford English Dictionary* mentions "cakes or loaves cut longwise in the shape of Naples biscuit".
Neat's tongue	a 'neat' is an ox, bullock, cow, or heifer.
Orangeado	candied orange peel variously spelt 'oringado' and 'orangado' in original.
Peal	a grilse i.e. a young salmon or sea trout.
Peck	a measure used for both liquid and dry goods equal to 2 gallons or 1/4 of a bushel (approximately 9 litres).
Peepers	young chickens or pigeons.
Pennyroyal	a herb, the smallest of the mint family.
Pickle cucumbers	gherkins. Could be used either fresh or pickled.
Pierce the gravy	meaning uncertain but probably 'pour off'.
Pipkin	a small pot or pan, maybe either earthenware or metal.
Pippins	a general term for many varieties of apple.
Pistaches	pistachio nuts.
Pottle	a measure equal to 2 quarts or half a gallon (a little over 2 litres).
Powdered	salted or pickled meat.
Prick them up	skewer them together.
Pannado	meaning uncertain, maybe derived from the Portuguese word 'punhado' - a handful.

Pride, Thomas	(d. 1658) served in Cromwell's army as a captain, then commanded a regiment at Naseby in 1645. In 1648, to frustrate an intended agreement with Charles I, he prevented about 130 MPs sympathetic to the King from entering the House of Commons in an event known as 'Pride's Purge'. Pride opposed Cromwell's appointment as King but accepted a seat in his upper house. He became rich enough to buy Nonesuch House in Surrey and was High Sheriff of the County in 1655. He died at Nonesuch in 1658.
Qualm	to boil.
Quartern	a quarter of various weight and measures.
Race of cinnamon	this is an error as a 'race' is a rootstock and the term is generally applied to ginger. Cinnamon is the bark of a tree so can only mean here 'stick cinnamon' or 'quill cinnamon'.
Race of ginger	a rootstock of ginger now usually known as 'root ginger'.
Raisins of the Sun	sun-dried grapes.
Red cock	red grouse, a reddish coloured gamebird.
Rivet	the liver of a fish, spelt 'revet' in original.
Rozin	rosin or resin - a gum obtained from plants and herbs or distilled from turpentine.
Sack	strong white wine probably imported from Spain or the Canaries.
Samphire	'Chrithmum maritimum' - a wild plant found growing on the seashore, mainly along the coasts of East Anglia. The aromatic fleshy leaves are salted, boiled, and pickled in spiced vinegar.
Scallops	a shellfish whose fan shaped shell is best known today as being that on which the 'Shell' Oil trademark is based. The white meat of the muscle

Mrs Cromwell's Cookbook

	is the part usually eaten today, but the prominent orange roe or 'coral' is sometimes included.
Scotch	score or cut.
Searsed, Searst	sieved or strained.
Send it smoking up	to serve it very hot.
Sindercombe, Miles	(d. 1657) a disenchanted Leveller and Republican who plotted with royalist agents to assassinate Oliver Cromwell. He was arrested after several failed attempts and committed suicide in the Tower of London in February 1657.
Sippets	small pieces of toasted or fried bread.
Skillet	a metal cooking utensil which has been described as a frying pan on legs. The same may also be used for any saucepan or stewpan.
Skirrets	a species of water parsnip, formerly much cultivated in Europe for its tubers which seemed to have been resembled dahlia tubers or potatoes in appearance.
Sliced nutmeg	it would seem almost impossible to slice a nutmeg, so this must refer to ground nutmeg.
Small beer	weak beer sometimes of poor or inferior quality, made from repeated brewing using the same mash.
Soak or soaking	to bake thoroughly.
Sops	bread dipped or soaked in some liquid.
Sorrel	a herb of the dock family with an acid, sour taste.
Strained almonds	crushed or pressed almonds. The modern equivalent would be ground almonds.
Sugar Peas	'mangetout' or edible podded peas.
Sweet butter	unsalted butter.
Sweet milk	fresh milk, not sour milk.
Trencher	a plate; sometimes a flat piece of wood on which the meat was served and cut up.

Tunnel	a funnel.
Verjuice	the acid juice of green or unripe grapes, crab apples or so the sour fruit.
Vial	another word for phial, a small glass bottle.
Walm	to boil.
Warden pears	an old variety of pear, supposed to have been grown originally by the monks of Warden Abbey, Bedfordshire.
Whalley, Edward	(c.1607 – 1675) was one of Cromwell's cousins and Parliamentarian soldier, rising to the rank of Major General. He sat as a judge on Charles I, so was obliged to leave the country at the Restoration with his son in law William Gough for exile in America.
While	until.
White	uncertain - could be white sugar.
Whole cinnamon	stick cinnamon or 'quill cinnamon'.
Winter-savory	a herb (Satureia montana) with a strong aromatic, peppery taste; good for gastric and digestive complaints. Leaves are also used in salami.

Most of the material in this glossary was originally compiled by Mary Liquorice F.L.A for the 1983 reprint of the Mrs Cromwell's Cookery Book, published by Cambridgeshire Libraries. Used with kind permission from them.

Glossary amended and updated by Stuart Orme, 2020.